BOUNCING BACK
2017 IN CRISIS!

HOW TO PREPARE FOR AND RECOVER

FROM LIFE'S GREATEST THREATS

Inspirational Stories from World-Class Athletes

Ronald L. Mann, Ph.D.

Mann Consulting Group

Bouncing Back 2017 in Crisis!

How to Prepare For And Recover From Life's Greatest Threats

ISBN 978-0-9710605-9-3

Library of Congress Control Number 2017902630

Mann Consulting Group
8 W Cochise Dr.
Phoenix, AZ 85021
310-387-5115
www.mannconsultinggroup.com

DEDICATION

To all those individuals who are making a serious and sincere effort to improve their lives and help those around them.

Acknowledgments

This book was a work in progress and various people helped it through its growth, evolution and development.

Merry Aronson of Merry Media has been a constant friend and source of support and inspiration. I thank her for always seeing the good and potential in the project and her unconditional love. If you need a great PR person, she is the one.

The athletes themselves made this work possible. They were generous, open and selfless in their willing to spend their valuable time and share their personal stories.

The road to finding the individuals to interview was an experiment in the two degrees of separation theory. One person knew someone who knew someone else. Don Dyer, Tom Satriano, Lena Evans, and Buddy Friedman helped in this unfolding network. I thank them for their help and kindness.

My friend Kathy Smith provided some very honest and timely feedback. I thank her for her honestly, clarity and gift of communication. Her contribution bought this work to another level.

Kathleen R. Kobak provided a priceless gift of editing to find errors that I never would have seen.

Following the writing of the first book, *Bouncing Back*, Coach Joe Taylor, asked me to write a book with him. He has become a friend and inspiration. His ability to bring wisdom and strength to the coaching of young men and women has transformed the lives of many young people.

TABLE OF CONTENTS

FOREWORD

By Coach Joseph D. Taylor

A few years ago I had the privilege of reading a book written by Ronald L. Mann, PhD. Dr. Mann is a Los Angeles Times best-selling author. The first book of "Bouncing Back" was a very inspirational book and I enjoyed the many stories of the athletes and how they managed the highlights and the lowlights of their careers.

I was nearing the end of my 40 years as a collegiate football coach, 30 as a head coach, and wanted to write a "giving back" career book. I reached out to Ron and he accepted my request to become my ghost writer.

He flew down to Tallahassee and we spent many days and nights together and wrote the book "The Making of A Champion: Success is an Inconvenience." Ron is one of those treasures that God puts in your life that comes along at the right time.

Speaking of the right time, "Bouncing Back: 2017 in Crisis!" is a must-read book. We are living in difficult times and maintaining our core values and a loving heart in the midst of chaos, conflict and turmoil is very challenging.

The contents of this book help us to prepare for and recover from life's greatest threats. Ron does a great job of identifying some of the more dangerous threats and what we need to do to manage and overcome their impact.

The first three are:

1) Our society needs to speak the truth – not "alternative facts."

2) Our society needs more respect for each other – less emotional reactivity to different points of view.

3) Our society needs to rise above fear and not react with hatred to new and changing circumstances.

When I read Ron's principle #1, those three or four mentioned threats were immediately addressed.

What is principle #1?

Spiritual realization can awaken within you a depth of wisdom, faith, and access to unseen forces that will support, guide and empower you in your most difficult times. (Find a man's spirit, also there you will find him).

The Lord blessed me with a very successful coaching career and the fundamental basis for that success came as a result of what Ron refers to as "principle #7."

What is principle #7?

Emotional Intelligence will determine how effectively you can react and respond in highly stressful circumstances.

1.   The importance of being able to accurately perceive the facts (reality) and respond to them.

2.   The importance of our ability to manage our emotional life and make good decisions (decisions are like elevators – they either take you up or they take you down).

3.   The importance of being able to manage strong emotion and not become impulsive (like "tweeting" at 3 a.m.)

This is a self-help book of guidelines for relevant coping and finding your way in these difficult times. Thank you, Ron, for writing this book. Our society will change for the better because of your spirituality and emotional intelligence. Please know how honored I am to call you friend and write this foreword.

Sincerely,

Joseph D. Taylor
Athletic Director
Virginia Union University
Mid-Eastern Athletic Conference Hall of Fame

INTRODUCTION

The ancient Chinese curse, "May you live in interesting times," continues to be upon us. When I published the first book in 2010, the country was in shock. The stock market had hit a low 6,443.27 on March 6, 2009 and swings of 500 points a day were common, home values had declined 10-40 percent across the nation, foreclosures were rolling across the country, job security had evaporated, 401(k) holdings were losing tremendous value, food prices were rising, health care costs continued to rise beyond reason, and international terrorism continued to threaten the security of all nations. Millions of Americans were worried, confused, lost, and anxious about their physical and economic security?

During the eight years of the Obama administration many of these realties became more stable. The economy was brought back from the brink of disaster, the auto industry was saved, home prices stabilized and rose again, massive foreclosures stopped, the stock market rose to 19,000 and panic was no longer in the air. FactCheck.org posted this in July 2016:

Since President Barack Obama first took office:

- The economy has added more than 10 million jobs, and job openings are at a 15-year high.
- The unemployment rate has dropped well below the historical norm, but long-term unemployment remains higher than at the start of the Great Recession.
- The buying power of the average worker's weekly paycheck is up 4.4 percent.
- Corporate profits are running 152 percent higher, and stock prices have soared.

- The number of immigrants caught trying to enter the U.S. illegally has dropped 53 percent.
- Federal debt has more than doubled, and annual deficits, after shrinking, are again on the rise.
- The home ownership rate has dropped by 4 percentage points.
- The number of Americans on food stamps is up 36 percent.
- Oil imports are down 53 percent, and wind and solar power have quadrupled.
- The number of people lacking health insurance has gone down by 15.2 million.

This is not to say that all is perfect in America. ISIS was born and international terrorism continues to be a serious problem. Syria became a human disaster and the Soviet Union began its aggressive moves by invading Ukraine. While the economy is better with the unemployment rate down to 4.9%, manufacturing is still moving overseas and our infrastructure of roads and bridges continues to be a mess. The Affordable Care Act (ObamaCare) helped millions get insurance, protect those with preexisting clauses and keep young people on their parents' policies, but there are still problems as rates and deductibles continue to rise. It definitely needs a fix.

So we moved from the brink of disaster to a more stable world, yet still troubled and far from perfect, but not destroyed, at least not here in America. We survived and made our way back—we Bounced Back. It is interesting to note that this was done without much help from the Republican Party. Their vision and policy was to stop President Obama from any accomplishments. They were the Party of NO! It is a wonder that the American people put up with their blockade and refusal to work and still give them a paycheck. If you owned a business and your employees announced that they were planning to come to work, but not do anything, would you fire them? Of course you would. We can only wonder how better we would be if the Republicans had decided to work for America, negotiate, and cooperate to actually make things better again.

History is a good teacher and we have always recovered. However, once again we are faced with massive change. We can keep our sanity and peace of mind if we remain hopeful and use the principles presented in this book. The American people were rightfully upset at the government for its dysfunction and gridlock. So they choose an outsider who painted a very dark and gloomy image of America in spite of many positive facts. But, who cares about facts anymore! We are off to a roller coaster start. Russia hacked us and may have affected the election, we really don't know about the real impact. We are not doing well with Mexico, travel from seven Middle Eastern countries is banned, our universities and corporations are issuing travel bans, people are on the streets in great numbers protesting, Russia and President Putin are being courted as an ally, and Steve Bannon, a man with White Supremacists inclinations, is a close adviser to our president. This is just after one week. Hopefully things will settle down, but the President's style does not suggest that.

Given our current life conditions there appears to be a great need to update the old *Bouncing Back* and relate it to our current time. I know you will find this information enlightening and helpful. Everyone has ups and downs in their lives. You are not alone. Life seems to be great and then something happens: your lose your job, you lose your home, someone close to you dies, you are affected by an act of terrorism, you are a victim of police misconduct, you get diagnosed with cancer, your daughter gets pregnant, or you lose all of your life savings and your 401-K. Many people today are in shock over the state of the world. While we have made some financial advances and an economic recovery over the eight years, many are still struggling. The world has changed: acts of terrorism have become commonplace, as a country, we don't feel as isolated and safe as we did, and individual acts of terrorism against common, everyday folks has risen. The future of the American economy and the world order are uncertain with the election of Donald Trump. We hope life will get better, but we really don't know what he will do and what the impact of his policies will be —— some have lost hope, others are blindly optimistic. Time will tell!

No matter whether your loss is personal wealth, health, loved ones or security, you might be living with more fear. Your inner life may be dark, fearful, and empty, or be filled with trust, faith, wisdom, and peace of mind. You have more control over your inner life than you may think.

This book is for those going through a major life change and may feel a catastrophic sense of loss or an increased sense of fear. Many people are not prepared emotionally or spiritually for a major life change. Anxiety, despair, hopelessness, and depression are often the result of such changes.

However, when your life falls apart, you don't have to follow! *Bouncing Back 2017 in Crisis!* is designed to give you a roadmap to help you prepare for and find solid ground during your most troubled times. The information presented here can help you emerge stronger as you go through the process of letting go and reconstructing your life.

Make no mistake; even though the material in the book is based upon interviews with world-class athletes, this is not a sport psychology book. It is much more. I have been fortunate to interview a number of world-class athletes who have shared their life stories and how they survived monumental life tests. We can learn a tremendous amount from these individuals and their stories apply to all areas of life. Of course, these stories and insights will help any athlete who wants to move to the next level in his or her career. However, the teachings and information here transcends sports. This is a book about surviving life's greatest challenges and disasters.

Most men do not search out self-help/personal development books. If you have a man in your life, a husband, father, brother, or son and you want to help them prepare for and cope with major life changes, give them this book!

I know these principles work because I have applied them in my own life and have also seen them work for others. I, like many people, had a financial meltdown when the economy tanked. One investment company, which handled a majority of my money, defaulted on a number of first trust deeds. The harsh reality was presented to me on November 15, 2008 that I had lost most of my income, which was based upon these 1st Trust deeds. I did have a moment of panic, but the depth of my spiritual experience — faith, trust and belief in myself kicked in. I kept calm, focused, opened to my intuition and lived each day at a time. I got to work and recreated a new life in Arizona after selling my home and downsizing. Life is good: no panic attacks, no depression, no heart attacks. I am once again financially stable and focused upon helping others. I developed a good Sport Psychology practice working with golfers, young and old. I was on the golf course almost everyday. I was happy and healthy.

Two years ago, suddenly, after an international trip to China and India my L4 disc blew out and created so much pain I could not stand for more than a couple of minutes. I could no longer work in the golf world, and after two surgeries and some rehab, I am good for everyday life. However, I no longer play golf and closed my sport psychology practice since I was no longer out on the course. I reinvented myself and created a new business out of a life long passion for design and technology — website development. In the last decade, I twice had major losses and found a way to maintain my mental health and prosper through the process.

I know others going through similar losses are not so fortunate. I have spoken with people who are overwhelmed with anxiety and depression. They appear to have few inner resources to help them survive and recover. Loss is tough, but it does not have to destroy you. It is possible to come out the other side more intact with a stronger sense of self.

I have had three members of my family die: my younger brother and both parents.

Death is another profound loss that can tear your heart out. I have relied upon these principles and "ways of being" to deal with the deaths of my loved ones as well. The principles in this book will help you with the most painful of losses. There are methods and ways of thinking that do support personal development and deeper realization that will empower you to be your best.

As I am sure you remember, we went through a devastating financial crisis in which fortunes were stolen or lost and individuals were forced to change and adjust in ways they never dreamed possible. I remember the TV interview in which Zsa Zsa Gabor's husband, Frédéric Prinz von Anhalt, was enraged over being swindled by Bernie Madoff. I could see the damage that his anger was doing to his health and spirit. How could anyone prepare for such radical shifts? These changes can prompt waves of fear, confusion, doubt, and uncertainty and these are not the mental and emotional states that lead to good coping skills and decision-making.

The financial situation still gets a lot of press these days. Creating new jobs and improving economic growth is a main goal for the new administration.

However, the shock of cancer, death, child abuse, divorce, and terrorism are daily occurrences. While these are devastating events, they do not have to destroy you.

Bouncing Back 2017 in Crisis! provides the wisdom, insight, and inspiration to help you cope and become psychologically and spiritually stronger through this process. You will learn eight fundamental principles that will provide a roadmap to guide you. The dictionary defines principles as "rules of right or good conduct." I do not offer these principles from a moralistic or pejorative position. These principles have been proven to work in life's laboratory. Read them and consider if anything suggested here might be of benefit to you. They have certainly provided a sold foundation for many successful people going through very difficult times.

The Eight Principles are exemplified in the personal stories of world-class athletes, many of whom are successful business people. You will learn the key elements that have allowed these individuals to succeed and conquer adversity in difficult and life challenging situations. Profound wisdom from psychology, spirituality and good common sense comes to life with these riveting stories. You will not only learn the key elements, but how to achieve those states as well! Each chapter will have a brief questionnaire to evaluate how you stand with each principle and a discussion, if you are interested, on how to enhance your performance and functioning in that particular area.

Individuals always need guidance, direction and inspiration to adjust and prosper. People often commit suicide because they do not have the internal strength and wisdom to survive devastating losses. This book is a guide for those who want to prepare for and emerge victorious, stable, healthy, and stronger! This discussion is integrated with the life stories of world-class athletes such as football legend Jim Brown, Olympic Gold Medalist Dick

Fosbury, baseball hero Doug DeCinces and baseball manager Buck Rodgers, Women's World Long Drive Champion Lee Brandon, boxing legends José Torres and Diego "Chico" Corrales. The stories are fascinating and inspiring.

Bouncing Back 2017 in Crisis! will share a vision regarding what you can do and how to accomplish it! Hopefully, you will be inspired to reach down deep and access your greatest potential. This information is field tested by the greatest players in the world as well as ordinary, every-day people. You will learn from and share the excitement, drama, successes and failures of our nation's greatest athletes.

The Eight Principles are derived from solid qualitative research over 40 years of clinical psychology, organizational development and spiritual practice. I have chosen to interview world-class athletes whose stories exemplify these Principles. As you read these inspiring stories, you will see that victory was not handed to these individuals. They all had to overcome obstacles, some more severe than others, and work hard for their success. They all could have given up, backed off, and lost faith in themselves. Each in their own way managed to find some inner resource and strength to persevere and ultimately succeed. Life is not necessarily easy and the road to success has many obstacles. These inspiring stories highlight what it takes to make it during tough times. We often find ourselves in difficult and challenging times. It seems to be the nature of reality. As such, we need a roadmap to find our way through. The following Eight Principles provide a foundation and guiding principles that can help anyone.

These principles are not airy-fairy qualities that promise instant success. I really dislike the simplistic promises that tell you all you have to do is "imagine" or "visualize" what you want and you will get it. Life is more complicated than that. If that were true, I would be sitting on a Billion dollar bank account! While these visualization techniques do help, they are not enough! I am going to give you real down-to-earth facts about real life that will work. You will get sound wisdom based upon years of practice. You may have to do some work and make some changes, but you will see the fruits from your efforts.

This book began as a sport psychology book, *The Magic of Peak Performance*. I had a contract with a major publisher that required me to get six household names. They obviously wanted to sell a lot of books based on name recognition. I was standing on the practice putting green at Riviera Country Club speaking with Steve, Tiger Woods' Caddie. Tiger was six feet away. Tiger was "working" and Steve made sure I did not bother him. Steve was not able to provide any help in my recruiting Tiger for the book. Tiger was obviously high on the list. Another day, back at Riviera Country Club I am standing next to Retief Goosen. I introduced myself to him and invited him to be part of the book. He looked to his left at an attractive woman and said, "Talk to my agent." I had a nice conversation with her that ended with, "I will think about it." She got back to me and said it was not a good time for Mr. Goosen to do the interview. Freddie Couples, same thing. He was presented with the request to participate and said not while he was playing. Andre Agassi had the same response. These all are great people, but were not available for this project. It appears that many of the current great athletes did not want to reveal their inner approach while they were competing. Some told me to talk to them when they retired. I sat on this material for a few months feeling a little discouraged, but I kept thinking about the interviews and the value of this material. Something in me kept bringing me back to this book. When the economy took a hit I was once again inspired to share this material. I saw the value for a "survival guide" during these very difficult economic times. While the material presented in this book goes far beyond economic issues, the world financial crisis was a motivating force to complete the writing of this work.

The world has changed over the last eight years, yet the need for personal strength and inner clarity remains the same — perhaps it is needed even more in today's violent world. This new book provides the same wisdom, but in a new voice that is more relevant to our current challenges.

I am eager to share this material because I know is will help you. I am very grateful to all those individuals who generously gave of their time to share these stories.

Chapter 1

The First Principle:

Spiritual Realization Can Awaken Within You a Depth of Wisdom, Faith, and Access to Unseen Forces that Will Support, Guide, and Empower You in Your Most Difficult Times

We begin with a discussion on spirituality because I believe it may be the most important. We need a strong foundation and inner strength to withstand life's challenges. Without a strong inner core, we hesitate and falter in the face of adversity. Just like an athlete needs a strong inner physical core to avoid injury, we need a strong inner spiritual core self that is authentic and inspired by something greater than our ego.

There is a tremendous difference between "*being*" and "*doing*." You can do all you want, but if you act from a shallow realm that lacks true realization of your spiritual nature, your actions will lack strength, inspiration, and personal power! Tough words and bravado do not withstand life's challenges. The other eight principles will depend upon a degree of inner realization. A strong inner realization is like a rudder that steers a ship. Your connection to Spirit can be a source of strength that guides you, heals you, and inspires others.

We begin with your spiritual development to prepare you when life gets tough. If you have not realized the gifts that consciousness holds, you will be lacking essential skills and qualities that you will need most in times of adversity. Prepare for life's challenges because they will certainly come. If you don't nurture your garden, don't expect anything to sustain you when life gets tough and confusing.

Let's be clear—I am not speaking about religious views and dogmatic beliefs. Spiritual awareness is a state of being that cuts across all religions and all beliefs. It is the direct experience of a greater presence that permeates all life. This presence may be call God, Jesus, Allah, Buddha, or whatever you like. It is tangible, wise, and loving.

Your doctor informs you that your latest lab tests and MRI are positive for a life threatening disease. There are several treatment choices with varying degrees of success. How do you decide what to do?

You have been betrayed and lied to and damaged by someone. You discover that your trust has been misplaced and the offending party shows no remorse over their actions. In fact, they seem to express a degree of disgust and contempt for you because you were so easily duped. How do you respond? Do you go into a downward spiral of anger and revenge in reaction? Or, do you find another way that does not cause you to become someone you never wanted to be?

You have an opportunity to make a lot of money and gain great power. However, you must lie in order to succeed. You believe you can get away with the lie. You need the money and want to have a better life. What do you do? What core values and beliefs determine your course of action?

A spiritual path is only useful if it helps you in every aspect of your life. Does the practice bring clarity in confusing situations? Do you find peace and strength when all your outer supports and resources have been stripped away? Can you access an inner strength in the face of adversity? Can you hold true to your own beliefs when others are pressuring you to act a certain way? Have you overcome the fear of death? Can you care about the welfare of others and make personal sacrifices to serve your family, community, country, or world? Does your spiritual life result in greater health and well-being? The spiritual practice and path I am referring to offers down to earth help and guidance for a better life — A way to overcome mistakes and create a better tomorrow. It is not about improvement in your next life or the rewards you will receive in heaven. It is about NOW and how you can help make this world a better place for yourself and others.

There is an additional boon to a spiritual life—wisdom. Direct spiritual knowledge is a function of the soul through an intuitive process. It is possible to experience the interconnection within all life. This direct knowledge removes the sense of isolation and separation that most people experience on a daily basis. This sense of unity creates a degree of comfort and support as you realize that God is in your heart, and we are all in this creation together. The eternity of the soul is revealed, and most fears fall away—especially the fear of death. More important than mere comfort, this Divine presence can have a tangible impact on your life and help you in the most amazing ways.

People often become offended or put off at the mention of spirituality because of prior negative experiences with traditional religious practices. Indeed, many have experienced religion as a restrictive force in their lives, because the particular practices and beliefs involved may have instilled fear, guilt, and shame. In this book, spirituality refers to one's direct, personal relationship with God without prescribing any particular path or way for sustaining that relationship or any one specific conception of God.

The many existing beliefs and concepts about the nature of Omnipresent Spirit suggest that God may be experienced in creation, with form, or in the absolute, formless state. This is not the issue here. Whether a person knows God as Christ, Buddha, Krishna, Allah, Mohammad, or whomever or whatever formless state of Being does not matter. Spirituality is that state of Being in which the unity and sacredness of all life is known and revered. Spirituality is the conscious knowledge that we are divine beings, a reflection and expression of the Divine, and the knowledge that the Holy Spirit moves through us all. How we define, conceive of, experience, and worship that sacred presence is an individual matter. In essence, all the great true spiritual traditions share the same goal—the direct personal experience of God.

Most people—especially in the West—are consumed by materialism: the belief that happiness will result as more stuff is accumulated (i.e., cars, houses, money, boats, clothes, TVs, girlfriends, husbands, etc.). Spiritual awareness reveals that true happiness is not found by accumulating more toys, but by self-realization—the awareness of the true nature of the Self that lies within. This inner knowledge and perception changes the goal of life from what you have to who you are. Your *State of Being* becomes more important than *What You Do*. Who you are while you are doing things becomes paramount. This is not the conventional perspective of most men in my generation. I hope the younger generation has a more enlightened view. Typically men look to money, sex, and power as definitions for personal worth and value. Unfortunately, love, compassion, and integrity are often seen as a sign of weakness. I am suggesting that a viable spiritual path promotes a sense of wholeness that integrates the masculine and feminine, the yin and yang, discipline and flexibility. Strength of body does not guarantee strength of heart! In a later chapter you will read an interesting discussion with football legend Jim Brown. You will be surprised to learn what he has to say about the source of his power.

One important consequences of economic meltdown can be a shift in values away from material consumption and financial wealth, as a measure of one's worth, to a realignment with deeper truths regarding integrity, honesty, service to others, and the value of community. As I write this new book, many people are angry and upset by their lack of wealth and security. They feel they have been left behind and want to be "first" again. The challenge that confronts us is — can we regain our economic security without losing our compassion and desire to help each other? Can we retain the wisdom that we are interconnected or do we allow ourselves to be fooled by the false promise that we can succeed at the expense of others? Can we sustain an open and loving heart and not be deluded into thinking we can succeed by attacking and blaming others? Being a bully and denying responsibility is not strength!

In the last few days a new concept has emerged, "Alternative Facts." We have seen an erosion in the respect for truth and a rise in the practice of misinformation. Our elected officials now make up whatever they want and become angry if the false information is confronted. Reality seems to have little impact. Observable facts and perceptions are no longer acknowledged as consensual reality. New facts and figures are presented from some alternative reality without any verifiable substance. Modern quantum physics does suggest that we may live in multiple alternative realities, and this seems to approach that. But this practice has no reasonable explanation beyond the desire for personal gain and power. Once again, how do we respond to this crazy-making reality? Are we prepared to address individuals who have little regard for truth and show no conscience about blatant attempts to manipulate others?

Let's Define Some Terms

When we lose our wealth, our health, or our security, we can be thrown into shock. Personal transformation typically does not come easily. The ego resists change, it does not want to let go — it likes to be in control. The ego is identified with the outer, superficial expressions of the self and the delusion of physical, material reality. Sometimes it takes a major personal loss or tragedy to shift our way-of-being away from the superficial aspects of the ego to the deeper, essential qualities of the Self.

In one of my previous books, *Sacred Healing: Integrating Spirituality with Psychotherapy*, I defined the different ways that the term "ego" is used. I think it would be helpful here to review that discussion.

The word ego is subject to great confusion and is used widely and loosely in both psychological and spiritual circles. In the psychological context, the ego performs a very positive function for the self. The ego is a hypothetical construct for the functions of thinking, perceiving, organizing, and integrating. It is psychologically important to have a strong ego in order to function well in daily life. Those with a weak ego structure have difficulty with their own emotional lives. They feel overwhelmed by their feelings, they are confused about their inner experience, and they have difficulty accurately perceiving outer reality without projecting their own unconscious material.

A strong ego allows you to confront the difficulties of life with confidence and have the strength and flexibility to be open to other people's thoughts and feelings without feeling threatened or overwhelmed. A strong ego—in this context—allows you to be intimate and to merge emotionally with another person without the need to create separation through conflict and anger as a way of re-establishing your sense of self. Knowing what you feel and think is a great asset. Knowing how to communicate that information to another person is a great gift in any relationship. A strong ego results from integrating all parts of your psyche—the light and the dark; the masculine and the feminine; and the various aspects of your personality, such as the child, adult, and parent. A strong ego allows you to let go and explore new territory when your consciousness begins to expand. If you have a very solid and well-integrated sense of self at a psychological level, then you can more easily allow for an inner shift of self-perception that includes a greater sense of your own being.

This leads to the other meaning of ego. From a spiritual perspective, ego is the aspect of self that experiences a separation from God. Ego consciousness believes that I am in total control of my life—that I am the total creator of my existence. The inherent limitation resulting from this notion is the absence of the full, integrated experience of your relationship with God. You end up feeling alone and isolated—abandoned and adrift in a changing and chaotic world. Your limited ego identity creates a contracted, separate, and reduced field of awareness. This contraction continues as long as your consciousness is identified with the outer manifestations of the self—the body, mind, emotions, and worldly possessions.

In the process of spiritual growth, you do not actually get rid of your ego. Rather, through spiritual practice and the gradual process of transformation, you shift the identification of your self beyond the ego to the soul through the transmutation of energy. This process of transformation allows you to transcend your attachment to and identity with the little self or ego. If you are interested, additional information about the process of transformation and techniques for expanding your consciousness are presented in a subsequent chapter on methods and techniques for change.

Stories From The Field
Lee Brandon

It is not uncommon to hear miraculous stories referring to the beneficial help that spiritual forces can play in daily life. Lee Brandon lived her life defying the odds—from surviving a near-fatal accident that rendered her left arm completely useless, to becoming the first woman ever hired by the NFL as an Assistant Strength Coach for the New York Jets, to winning the 2003 Women's World Long Driver Invitational Championship Safeway Classic and winning the RE/MAX 2001 World Long Drive Championship in her rookie year—having never hit a long ball in her life until the spring of 2001! .

Lee Brandon has been a client and friend. I began working with Lee one year after she had won the 2001 RE/MAX Long Drive Championship and before she won the 2003 Safeway Classic. I have found her to be one of the most inspirational people I have ever met or had the pleasure to coach. Her work ethic, high moral standards, and enlightened world-view set her apart from most athletes I have ever met. She has a depth of spiritual realization that emanates from her.

Lee and I discussed her performance, and I asked her about the will, asking, "So, would you say the power of the will has a lot to do with the capacity to succeed in life?"

She initially spoke about decision-making but expanded her thoughts as we continued to discuss this important topic. Please note where she ends up with this discussion on the "will."

"So to me, the power of decision or the power of goal-setting is more powerful than my powerful will, because to me, once I have a goal, then there is no option to abandon that goal. You might fall short of it, but the only option is to have a goal or not to have a goal.

18

"So to me, the power of goal-setting, the power of being in the moment, the power of being resourceful, the power of education, the power of preparing—all of these things create what I guess would be my manifestation of will. Others might view this as will; but to me, they are keys to success. I think that every great human being I've ever met ... Bob was great (more will be said about Bob Weiland in later chapters), because he kept putting his hands in front of each other. He had a goal. He just had to wake up and just keep pursuing that goal. Some people would view him — looking at him, you'd have to say he has an inordinate amount of human willpower. But to talk to him, you would just say, 'He just had the goal, and that was it.' And I guess, in my mind, it was always about trying to find a goal that matched my talent. I knew that quitting wasn't an option, so I guess—if that's defined as will, then I guess I have some. But to me, success is based on certain steps— perseverance and resourcefulness. I can't leave out close contact with your higher power or what you believe in, because I think without that, I wouldn't have made it through certain things if I didn't believe in something larger than my own will."

COMMENTARY

Lee is explaining a very, very important issue here—attunement with a higher power. The ideal is to align your will with the Divine Will, or whatever you want to call it. The recovery community talks about finding a higher power in anything that works for you. Everybody has to start somewhere— even if it is your Harley. The point is, if you can become inspired by some greater sense of Being and invite that feeling or presence into your heart and life, then you can become empowered to accomplish more than you might think possible. Aligning your will with the Divine Will gives you a great degree of power because you are motivated by inspiration. This inner alignment creates a degree of clarity and awakens a collaborative relationship with the Divine that results in what seems to be mystical help. Wait till you hear what Dick Fosbury has to say about this.

The hidden power of consciousness is important to understand. At the quantum level, there is an energetic field that orchestrates reality. The nature of vibrational energy determines how matter is shaped—different frequencies create different physical structures.

Your individual thoughts also create an energetic field that affects your personal world. Your presence—or your energy—has an impact on animate and inanimate objects around you. People are affected by your presence—plants, animals, and even computers respond to the very nature of your being. As we will discuss in later chapters, Dr. Emoto from Japan has done some very interesting studies with ice crystals and thought. He has shown that different types of thoughts actually create distinctly different patterns in ice crystals. Happy, joyful, loving thoughts create beautiful symmetric patterns, and negative, hostile thoughts create ugly, misshapen patterns.

As you align your will with the Divine Will, you increase your ability to hold harmonious frequencies that result in the manifestation of specific intentions. Creation began with a thought from God, and your thoughts and intentions have the power to manifest as well. There is a divine perfection and order to life. Your will can be aligned and attuned with the Divine, which increases your power to manifest everything you need. Manifestation begins in thought and then condenses down into solid form. You can become a compelling force to bring things into creation. Paramahansa Yogananda, in his *Autobiography of a Yogi*, shares some rather amazing stories in this regard.

You are invited to look at his book and his stories about Mahavatar Babaji for an eye-opening view at the possibilities we possess.

It is important to understand these deeper truths in today's challenging times. We have all lost something in our lives: money, elections, power, health, etc. We need to create new opportunities and possibilities and most effectively respond to the situations at hand. It is difficult to manifest jobs, money, and connections even in the best of times. However, when you are in tune with these subtle realms and consciously use the power of your spiritual nature, you have an added advantage and a hidden power. You will find that you can accomplish more with less effort. You will find that you will meet the right people for connections and networking, and new opportunities will be drawn to you. It is imperative to keep positive and not let negative thinking and negative influences rob you of your peace and impair your ability to attune with the Divine.

BACK TO THE INTERVIEW WITH LEE

"How do you connect with that something that's larger? Do you have any method for doing that?"

"I'm a big believer in prayer. I believe in prayerful states. I'll find myself talking at certain points, or being grateful. Like, 'Look at the beautiful tree.' I'll just find myself driving and looking at things and not talking to myself, but almost talking to a higher power and being grateful to still be alive, and just trying to be in a grateful, thankful place and trying to be open for opportunities. And I think that has allowed me to move forward many days when I felt like—you just don't feel like you can overcome the inertia. What is that quote? 'We don't sing because we're happy, we're happy because we sing.' I think, in my case—some days, on the days that I don't feel like I'm happy, if I can re-attach myself to what I know, the grassroots of what is me. It goes all the way back to that life changing experience when I lost my arm. I get back in touch with that; then I know that higher power is there. It's like a foundation I always have. It's like a center that I find with my thoughts and with every breath. It's something that's just there. It's not even something I question—ever. If somebody asks me to prove it—you can't necessarily prove a feeling, but it's something that was a gift I was given that forces me to believe in something bigger than myself. Because there's no way in my heart I could ever dismiss that."

"How have you overcome adversity?"

"I think I have a lot of techniques to overcoming adversity. I think, again—everything, in most cases in my life, most everything goes back to LCD; what I call LCD, the lowest common denominator. I go back to my primary reason for being alive. Why am I here? And it doesn't allow room in there for me being depressed. There's not room in there. There's room for being realistic, which often comes with disappointment, but there's never room for me wallowing in it. There's room to assess it, there's room for me to feel it and mourn it, but not to be stuck there. Because to me—I've seen so much motion in my life. I've come from nothing, I've seen everything, and I've gone back to nothing. And I think in knowing that life comes with those dips—that's just realistic, and trying not to be in a deluded place.

"I think da Vinci said it best. I studied this in college. In da Vinci's scheme of things—because da Vinci was quite a scientist and quite a philosopher— that he called it the 'gap of tragedy'—the gap between what is ideal in our mind and the gap between what is real. What really is happening? What really can occur? What really can I do, vs. what ideally I think I can do — who I really think I am, and what I think my will is. So in my heart, I always do my very best to try to not get lost in between what's real and what's ideal. Because that gap, in da Vinci's scheme of things, was called the gap of tragedy. And I think a lot of people fail, because what's ideal and what is real don't match. So my entire life has been spent trying to narrow down that gap and modify my ideals and explore my real—explore what I really can do. I didn't really know what I could do, and in my golf swing, I don't know if I could really … is 350 out of my range? I don't know. I haven't explored that thought. My ideal would be 352. I think I can do it. But is that realistic? I don't know.

"But in that interim, there's a gap of tragedy. But am I going to be disappointed if I only hit, like, 274 that I hit in the finals this year? Yes, I'm disappointed! I didn't lay my best shot on it. I didn't beat myself; I didn't up my best. I know I didn't deliver the best thing to the back of the ball. But after the world championships, you walk away and you say, 'I have to manage that.' My ideal was much higher, but I can't get lost in that gap of tragedy, and I think that is how I manage my dips.

"Because that hiccup—coming in fourth when I know I'm better than that, and I couldn't beat myself up about it. What are you going to do? In that moment, it just didn't come together for me. I did the best I could. I laid the best swing I had at that moment on the ball, and that was it. I've been in worse places. I've been in a hospital bed recouping from a lost arm. I think when you've felt the worst, and you know that hiccups happen in life—we can't be spoiled and think that our ideal is going to happen all the time. It just doesn't."

COMMENTARY

Another way to think about the gap of tragedy is the difference between one's potential and one's capacity. Just because we have the potential to accomplish something does not necessarily mean we will be able to do so. Perhaps our capacity will not reach our potential; however, it is important to try nevertheless. The important thing is not to be attached to the results if we come up short.

There is a very instructive Sufi story from Indris Shaw:

There was once a devoted student who served his Master for his entire life. He would travel with his Master from town to town and take care of all his needs. One day, his Master asked him to go into the nearby town, enter a bar, and find a man playing the guitar. His devotee, as always, followed his Master's request and entered the bar to find a man playing the guitar. However, this man was really a drunkard. The devotee thought, "Who can understand that ways of the Master? I don't know what he would want with this man." Nevertheless, being a devoted disciple, he explained to the man that his Master wanted to see him and took him back to the river where his Master waited. Once back at the camp, he watched his Master invite this man onto his blanket. Once the man stepped on the blanket, it began to rise. It became obvious to the devotee that his Master was making his final accent to heaven with this drunkard. He was outraged. He shouted, "How can you take him? I devoted my entire life to following your teachings and serving you. You should be taking me!"

His Master looked down and replied, "You don't have the capacity."

Obviously, it is important to realistically assess what you can actually do, even though you may hold some lofty goals. How can you live in such a paradox without continued frustration and a sense of failure? The answer is an attitude of non-attachment. The ideal goal is to act with 100 percent effort but not be attached to the outcome—accept what happens when you know you tried your best. This is not necessarily an easy state to obtain, but the rewards are great when you can. This is also an important attitude for parents and coaches to maintain.

As a parent, it is best not yell and berate your child if he or she brings home a B grade if you know your child tried in that class. If your team loses to a better team, as their coach, it can be more helpful if you do not berate them for their loss. This attitude of non-attachment allows you to try hard and still have a sense of positive self-worth if you don't always reach your goals. Furthermore, if your child or team did not seem to be putting out 100 percent effort, then your job is to find out why. Talk with your son or daughter and uncover the reasons for the breakdown in effort. Be smart, help to educate and inspire, and you will be teaching a self-coaching method that will last a lifetime.

This attitude of non-attachment is very relevant to our current times. People's lives have been turned upside down. When you have lost elections, health, wealth, or security, it is easy to get depressed and feel hopeless. However, if you can make the adjustment, keep a positive state of mind, and let go of the attachment to the things that have defined you, you have a much better chance of coming out the other side stronger and whole. You will also be able to see new solutions and new opportunities. If you try to hold on to the way your life was, you will be stuck in a dark hole of despair. In order to extricate yourself from the gap of tragedy, you must look to the present and face reality. You will find new energy and discover new opportunities when all your energy and focus is in the present.

Often, we need a major catastrophic event to shake our identification with the ego. Oftentimes we have to hit bottom before we find the motivation to act. Loss creates a great opportunity for spiritual growth, because we have to dig deep to find a new motivation and remember our purpose in life. The recent election of Donald Trump has caused a great deal of distress for millions of Americans. However, just one day after the inauguration, four hundred thousand people in Washington and several million people worldwide turned out for a massive, successful, non-violent protest that could empower a new generation. People need to keep active and persevere if they want to achieve the change to desire. One action is never enough.

ON PRESENCE

I asked Lee Brandon, "How did you learn to stay in the moment? You're very present. As I look in your eyes, you don't wander off. You know, some people—you look in their eyes, and they're darting around; they can't even look at you, and you can see their mind's dancing all over the place. And you're very here, you're very focused, you're really calm—dynamic, but not in a frenetic kind of way. How did you find this state—how did you come to it?"

"That's a good question. I don't know. My only guess is that sometimes when you've been through such horrible things … everybody in their life has been through horrible things. But sometimes the people who have been through the hardest things have had to find a way to come back to a center place, and then after that, everything else sort of pales into insignificance.

"And I feel like you're asking some very important questions. I think that the average person would never even go and think these thoughts, or even think about wanting to explore becoming better, because our life is so fast, and frantic, and fast cars and fast food and lose weight quick and everything is about fast results and feeling better fast, and that's not necessarily—again, that's that gap of tragedy between what's ideal, what we ideally want, what we're Hollywood-sold, and what's real. I think that when I go to a real place and discuss real things, it has its own depth. Sort of like being on a deep river—there are no rapids when you've had that tumultuous kind of stuff; it's a deep place. It has to be calm. It has a tremendous amount of years and depth of pain and experience behind it, and you can't give somebody that. That's why losing is so important. That's why, when people lose things, and they make it through that, it gives you that depth to be able to have such greater empathy and depth of understanding and greater appreciation for great things when they really hit—is sort of my thought."

I said, "You know, it occurs to me, too—is that through that whole process of tragedy, adversity, and loss, when you come out the other side and you're still there, you have a clear sense of self that's not identified with those outer things or the transitory state you're in, whether it's up or down—and you've been up, you've been down, and when it all passes through, you're still there in the moment … I know for me, it's a way of learning how to stabilize in some deeper self that isn't so reactive to moment-to-moment transitory situations."

"I think it forces you to explore parts of your inner being that would never be strengthened otherwise—trial by fire. And ultimately that just reminds me of the story of what I call the crucible—these little stories that I cling to. These brass foundries—if you walk in, these huge, huge, thousand-pound crucibles are what hold the brass. And you walk up to one that's on fire, and you take a sledgehammer to it, and you hit, and you hit it, and you hit it repetitively—it doesn't make a dent in that crucible, that big pot. It wouldn't even make a dent.

"But you could take a small hammer over to one that's empty, and tap it when it's cold, and it shatters into a thousand pieces. So I believe people are very similar. When they're full of what they love and they're on fire, they're very deep, and they can withstand more. But when we're shallow, or when we're cold, and haven't explored our insides, or we're not hot about anything, or we're just timid or lukewarm—that's when we break easily into a thousand pieces."

"That's a great metaphor for life."

"Yeah. So I always go back to—when I'm feeling timid and cold, to refilling my soul and going back to what lights me on fire. And I've shared with you some of those things. Because if you're on fire, I'm telling you—you can't be broken. Even the biggest losses can't break you."

FURTHER INSIGHTS INTO THE MYSTERY OF CONSCIOUSNESS

DICK FOSBURY

One of our esteemed athletes in this collection is Dick Fosbury. He holds a gold medal in High Jump from the 1968 Summer Olympics held in Mexico City. He set a new Olympic record (2.24 meters/7 feet 4.25 inches) with his revolutionary style now know as the Fosbury Flop. Aspects of his story will be discussed in other chapters regarding self-belief and individuation. He continued to explore his own approach and allowed his style to naturally unfold in an intuitive way. To his credit, he did not let others deter him, in spite of the Russian and European coaches assuring him that his technique would never be successful!

Something rather wondrous happened to Dick at the Olympic games. I will let him explain it in his own words. Prior to this discussion, Dick and I were talking about life force energy and consciousness. It was actually near the very end of our interview that Dick shared this story with me. It took about forty-five minutes to get to this deeper, personal experience. The written account of this conversation loses something. Dick was really very open with me and telling me something that he may not have told a lot of people. He was really struggling to make sense out of something that he could not explain. His experience of being so high and getting over the bar was clearly a transcendental moment for him—not just in terms of physical accomplishment but also the mental state he was in. Something bigger than him helped him to accomplish this, and he did not know how to explain or even describe what he clearly felt. Moreover, Dick Fosbury is a very intelligent and articulate man. This experience was definitely something out of his normal state of being. I was very touched by his account of that winning jump.

I believe his Olympic experience exemplifies the mystery of life and how Spirit does support us. We can be helped by unseen forces to accomplish great things. It is my experience that we are not alone.

It is difficult to conceptualize about his experience. Different people with different belief systems would probably describe it within their particular paradigm. It is safe to say that something transcendent of the typical human experience occurred in that moment. Some greater forces were at work that opened the door for an entire life change—not just winning the gold, but also opening doors for an entire lifetime of service to humanity. If we consider spirituality to be a greater connection and sense of unity with life, then I think this could be considered a spiritual gift.

Dick Fosbury said, "One of the things that I'll never forget was that feeling. Once I was on my winning height, once I was over the bar and there was space between my body and the bar, and I had this sensation of amazement —and just surprise—that I had actually gotten in that place, because I never really knew whether I could do that or not, and once I had cleared the bar, I knew that I had at least taken the lead, if I had not won the gold.

"I have never been able to figure out how I did it. Just from the circumstance of knowing where I came from and being a good athlete—but never a great athlete—and finally reaching that place that was at the highest level of competition and which I really thrived on, and it was just always amazing to me that I had actually reached there. I always felt, for some reason, that something else put me there, and I didn't know what it was."

I asked, "Can you explain anything more about this 'something else'?"

"You know, I'm not sure. It's always been a mystery to me. I've always felt that there was something else that guided me to that place at that moment. That it was just beyond … it was just beyond me. And it was unexplainable. It was beyond anything that I had ever experienced or sensed. And it's always been a puzzle. Well, it's more than a puzzle; it's always been a mystery—something that I've never experienced since. It's certainly a peak experience; it's an ultimate moment, but I could never really grasp the why and the how. I just felt like something else put me here. There's something beyond me. There's something beyond me as an individual that carried me there. I didn't feel that strong. I didn't feel that strong to get there, and yet there's something that gave my body the strength to—not just to jump that high, but to actually have the perfect technique, and the perfect approach, and everything worked. It was such a mystery that I actually convinced myself that I would never do it again—which I didn't. But you know—it didn't matter. It did not matter in the least, because I got there. And I experienced that, and I don't really know why, other than it's been such a gift. It's taken me places around the world. I've met amazing people; I get to talk to people and teach kids and do things way beyond where I thought I was going to go. So it's been a great gift, but there's that place that was just a mystery!

More on Life's Mystery
Jim Brown

It is important to note that on several occasions, my discussion with these great athletes turned to spiritual matters. As we became more comfortable with each other and I shared more of my interests and background, they began to share stories that I do not believe they typically discussed in other interviews. My interview with Jim Brown is a good example of this. I had just mentioned my interest in alternative healing, meditation, and consciousness in our conversation. Here is what transpired:

"Well, I thought you're just hanging in the sports thing," said Jim Brown. "That's a part of my life. I can feel a lot of things."

"When did that first open up for you?" I asked.

"Pretty much been all my life. You know, it's pretty much been all my life, but I was emphasizing the preparation on my work and all those things because of the practical side of it, which makes you more in tune to receive these particular gifts. And they are gifts, because I can relate to some people … I can relate to a lot of people if I want to. You know, I can just do it. I can transfer, you know, goodness. I can make a person feel goodness when I really care about them without a lot of words."

Commentary

Once again, we are back to a discussion regarding consciousness and its impact on another individual. When Mr. Brown states that he can transfer his goodness, I believe he is referring to the process where his life force energy, or prana, is emanating to another individual. This phenomenon is very common in the healing arts like Qi-Gong, Reiki, therapeutic touch, or other energetic healing methods. The heartfelt energy of the soul can be transferred to another. It is simply the sharing of subtle energy forces that are generated by a conscious individual.

In more profound experiences of healing, when major illnesses are spontaneously reversed, the issue of God's grace becomes more relevant. Those who have the greatest gift actually take no personal ownership of this power. The gift is clearly seen as a gift from the Divine as the giver serves as a vehicle through which this energy flows. This is a very interesting discussion that you can find in my book, *Sacred Healing: Integrating Spirituality with Psychotherapy.*

BACK TO THE INTERVIEW

I said to Jim Brown, "I believe that we have an energetic presence about us. You have a very, very strong one. It is very tangible!"

He answered, "I just met with Jim Sheridan, the director, and 50 Cent [Curtis Jackson]. And he basically felt my spirit. I projected it to him, because I appreciate his level of intellect. I was able to project that appreciation to him, so he felt that; he knew I understood what he was saying, and he knew I appreciated it. When I went in today, he basically said that. I could call on that almost silently—just by the attention I might pay to what he's saying. I can feel a change in mood in a person just like that without moving, even when I am out of the room. I almost know how they're going to come in, you know.

"I think the people that have it strongest … what I was going to talk about, I speak for myself. I have to be kind of pure. You know? I have to be, like, positive in the sense to be able to pick up. I can't bullshit with them or anything like that — I can't fake it, I have to feel and leave myself open to it.

Sometimes, if I want to figure if someone's telling the truth, I just go into this state where I let it come to me.

"You know, just open my mind and see what comes in. I don't try to make anything come in, but I see what comes. And in most cases, it's right—and sometimes I don't want it to be that way, but you know … so I've learned quite a bit about that. And I believe that if I'm pure enough, and strong enough, I can make that thing move. I believe that if I can visualize … I believe that if a person can visualize putting something together, that's almost a form of moving it anyway."

"Do you think it's teachable?" I asked. "To help people to develop that intuitive consciousness so they can have greater impact in their life?"

"Yes, I think that you can teach a person to deal with—not to be afraid of honesty. See, I don't think you can teach it. I think there's a step where a person will be in a state of mind to have it where it's possible. What happens, in my opinion—society has so much bullshit in it that it clogs up what we're talking about. It just overpowers it because, you know, the President's (George W. Bush) talking about the goodness of being in Iraq. And you have to try to believe that it's good to be in Iraq. And, shit, I don't see nothing good about being in Iraq. But the propaganda machines are rolling out, rolling out, rolling out, rolling out. And how does a person get pure in this society? So if you're being inundated with bullshit that sounds good from the top all the time, it clogs up your ability to truly be sensitive. See, it's like trying to be popular rather than being honest. It's like selling out for money.

"So there are not very many people that are walking around that are pure enough to truly feel any damn thing. And you can have a conversation with most people, and they don't want to talk for real, they want to talk about some preconceived bullshit. You know, keep personality score. 'Oh, Jim, I really like …' They ain't even listening to me. You know, you're not even listening, man. I'm trying to tell you something. I'm trying to talk to you as a human being, but you're not even listening. So you're just telling me things you think I want to hear, because you have this image of me. But if we talk, and I can understand you, that's of mutual respect.

"So, you can teach it, I think, through dealing with truth—and, like, getting a person to be able to deal with truth, which happens to be with their feelings. In our courses that we teach, feeling's become a big part of it. Not right and wrong, but how you feel.

COMMENTARY

I am struck by the current relevance of Jim Brown's comments on the nature of politics and the level of "bullshit" that is dished out. Truth and honesty are a foundation for spiritual development. It is said that our word develops power to manifest when we only speak the truth. Jim Brown also said that his ability to remain clear and intuitive becomes enhanced as he lives more in truth. I am personally concerned that "truth" is no longer seen as an important factor and words are not given much value—say whatever you want and never be held accountable. If someone attempts to hold you accountable, just attack them, appears to be the norm. This is a recipe for personal and spiritual disaster. Words do matter and karma cannot be avoided. Be careful what you say because you will be held accountable in the end.

I deeply appreciate Jim Brown's willingness to reveal his mystical and spiritual nature. He has intuitive capacities and consciously uses his spiritual power to positively influence those around him. His energy is quite tangible. It is easy to believe he can have a strong impact on another when he so chooses. We live in a cynical world that often attempts to dispel and invalidate these deeper truths about the nature of human consciousness. Jim Brown is a man of reputation and credibility who demonstrates that a man can be strong and powerful and still have a connection to his heart and soul.

The brief discussion on how to teach this reality is important. The reality is that consciousness is not a technique; it is the result of personal development that honors truth. We all have the potential to be very conscious, to be deeply intuitive, and to powerfully impact our environment. These powers or gifts are inherent in our nature; but in most individuals, they are clouded over by an over-identification with the ego—what I want, what I need, and what I think. The process of getting clear results is an internal awareness of these profound and powerful states. There are various methods for getting clear. All spiritual traditions have processes. The bottom line is that you have to clean out the turmoil of emotional conflict—especially anger, rage, jealously, fear, and envy. You have to learn how to get out of your mind, let go of judgments, and release preconceived ideas so you can actually experience reality—not what you think reality is or should be! If you can quiet your mind, resolve emotional conflicts, internalize your energy, and open your heart, then a different world becomes available. I do provide actual methods to accomplish this in later chapters.

As Jim Brown stated, there is too much bullshit going around. Many people do not want to hear the truth, because it makes them uncomfortable. The spiritual path—the path of awakening—is for the brave and courageous. It is not easy to confront one's inner demons, but the rewards are enormous.

I think it is very important to realize that the world's greatest football player is a mystic, and his conscious awareness of his deeper spiritual, intuitive nature has something to do with his success and his ability to help others.

In our society, we typically focus upon outer accomplishments and physical or material success. Perhaps one of the great lessons we can learn from this interview is that one of the biggest, strongest men in our society, who is admired by millions, also has a deeper, internal, subtler side that is worth understanding and emulating.

ON THE HUMAN SPIRIT
JIM BROWN

"Once you discover the human spirit, then that's where your success lies—inside that spirit. And it's awesome when you're able to touch it. You're a difficult person to handle, because you're not in things for the same reason a lot of people are in it for. Man, the thing that you really want to do is to help a lot of people. So ultimately, having the human spirit, you have to be pure enough to open yourself up for all the things that you can't necessarily explain—the purer you get, the more of it you can absorb, and the more that you can put out there.

"Then, like the gang-bangers that I deal with, I never just tell them what to do. We have a curriculum they go through, and I have a relationship with them, and they are taught how to make decisions and set goals, but I don't tell them what to do!

"I've had gang members come in here since 1988; never had a gun pulled on me, never had anybody touch me. And it's only through spirit. It's only through that. But you don't brag about it. You appreciate it, because you understand it.

"I ran into a guy tonight. And I didn't remember him. And he was, like, expecting me to react, and I didn't react. And he went and he parked my car, and he came back. And I was worried about saying to him, 'Well, who are you?' And he didn't exactly tell me, and I was rushing, so I was kind of rude. And he was, like, ex-gang member had been in prison that I used to deal with a lot, but he cut his hair and everything. He thought I said, 'What do you want? Do you want something?' He said, 'I don't want nothing,' he was like, boom, boom!

"And then I turned around, and I said, 'Oh, man, I didn't recognize you,' because I hadn't recognized him. It was a guy named Baby Huey, who was someone that I used to have at the house, and I used to take him down to the racquetball court, and he said, 'Yeah, I want to see you to thank you for the things you've done for me.'

"I was so happy that I recognized him, but I was being real—I was doing the best I could do with a guy I didn't know who seemed to know me. But it came through, and I was so damn glad. But I was being honest—but it wasn't good. It would have been nice if I did recognize him, but when I did, I was honest, which was good. And I was riding home, I was thinking about it, but I know he'll call, and we'll get together, because he had this smile on his face.

"I react to goodness real well. I respect kind people, gentle people, way more than anybody that's going to intimidate me. You know—just the opposite. A lot of times, our society, there's intimidation factor—somebody's rich, or they're powerful, but no. I pick up on the Spirit—makes you relevant forever.

"The greatest experience I had after football was when I did a book and went to Ohio for the book signings. And families would come up that had enjoyed each other while they were enjoying me play. So I realized for the first time that fans had a hookup, and a lot of them were genuinely fans, because it went beyond one of them just watching you play. But they would have an event of the family going to the game—then you were the star, and they had a good time with each other and had a good time watching you. And that really computed to me when they were standing in line. Before, I never understood it. I never really bought the fan concept. I thought it was just kind of superficial. But they—and I was very glad for the revelation, because then I had a great appreciation of what was going on. I didn't know that was going on while we were playing—father and son, grandfathers, mothers, daughters. So I was learning. I was learning.

"If a human being gets pure enough, there wouldn't be damn anything we couldn't do. If we had the ability to internally go to the right state, we would probably fly."

Final Comments

Jim Brown seems genuinely sincere about his desire to honestly help others. He shares a striking sense of humility as he acknowledges the source of this power: a gift from Spirit.

When I first arrived at Mr. Brown's home for the interview, he informed me that he was very busy and only had about fifteen minutes to spend with me. An hour and a half later, we finished our conversation. I can only assume it was my sincere desire to get to know him and my personal interest in the deeper aspects of life that motivated him to spend the time with me. He did often say during the interview, "I thought you were just interested in football." He had no idea that I was interested in spiritual matters.

Jim Brown tells us that honesty, sincerity, and the power of the human spirit can accomplish great things. He is certainly a living example of what he teaches. With regards to the power of the human spirit, I have an interesting story to share.

A few years ago, I was attending an annual spiritual retreat for the Self Realization Fellowship (SRF). This organization was founded by Paramahansa Yogananda. He came to America in the 1920s to teach the principles of yoga—meditation, love of God, and service to humanity. The SRF has become a worldwide organization. The yearly event, simple called the Convocation, is held in downtown Los Angeles at the Bonaventure Hotel. There are usually between three and five thousand individuals who attend.

One evening, a monk who had studied with Yogananda, Brother Anandamoy, wanted to take a walk outside of the hotel. It was in the evening. Brother Anandamoy was in his seventies and was one of the most respected and revered disciples of Yogananda. As you might imagine, a seventy-year-old man dressed in an orange robe late at night might not be perfectly safe on the streets of downtown Los Angeles. The brother had a couple of bodyguards for protection. The men all were advanced black belts in various forms of martial arts.

After a few minutes on the street, a seemingly psychotic individual approached the group and became rather verbally intrusive. The bodyguards told him to back off, but he was not deterred. He continued to move toward Brother Anadamoy, and the guards were about to go into action. At this point, Brother Anadamoy told them to stop. Brother simply looked at this individual, and by some unseen force had some impact on this troubled man. All of a sudden, without any apparent outer reason, the man said, "I am so sorry, please forgive me. God bless you." He then turned around and walked away.

As Jim Brown has said, the power of the human spirit gives us strength and helps us to accomplish great things—"If a human being gets pure enough, there wouldn't be damn anything we couldn't do. If we had the ability to internally go to the right state, we would probably fly." Maybe that is what happened with Dick Fosbury—he just flew over the bar!

Additional Thoughts on Overreacting

I want to share one final thought on the value of a spiritual consciousness and the fruits of meditation. In the last week we have seen President Trump sign several Executive Orders that are questionable with regards to the Constitution and House support. President Trump loves to get people worked up to create drama, chaos and confusion. He already has millions of people on the street, all around the world, in protest to his decrees. It appears that we live in an era of social action. Social media allows for instant connects and people see the power of public demonstrations. Public demonstrations can be a powerful and positive force, especially if they are non-violent and serve to inspire and empower people. However, it appears that we are in for a long ride with President Trump over the next four years and do you want to be in emotional chaos and reaction every day for the next four years? Just because President Trump tweets something or says something, you do not have to react with fear and outrage and start running around! Yes, you can take action if you do not agree with what he is doing, but you don't have to act from a highly emotionally reactive place, that will burn you out! You will never last the four years. Use your spiritual practice to develop some detachment from your emotions when you need it.

Many years ago in the 1980's I had a Swami from India staying in my home. He loved to create drama. He had a group of loyal followers in my home everyday. He would declare, "Pack my bags." Everyone jumped at his instant demand and went to work. Ten minutes later, "Unpack my bags." Now the group quickly got to work with the new task. This went on and on, "pack—unpack." My home now felt like a psychiatric center. I told these people that they had to stop reacting to what Swamiji was saying. They told me, "But, this is what he wants." I said, "I don't care what he wants. Stop reacting!" They could not stop reacting and I could not allow my home to become an insane asylum. I started sending people home, one by one, until I was the only one left with the Swami.

Don't let President Trump drive you crazy with every tweet and thought. Your mental health may be at stake here over the next four years. Of course, if you like what he is saying then this will not be a problem for you. I suspect you will be very happy, but you might now get angry with all the people who do not agree with you and take to the streets to protest. Now you are in reaction to those in reaction. You do not have to be part of this drama. Please do stay politically active, speak up, and honor your values, but you don't have to be an emotional whirlpool filled with anger, contempt, and judgment while you are expressing yourself.

SELF-ANALYSIS—SPIRITUALITY

Answer the following questions: True or False

1. I believe that the mystery of life is fully grasped as one learns to surrender to its many challenges.

2. I believe in a Higher Power that guides and directs the universe.

3. I feel in touch with my soul.

4. I have a desire to help others.

5. Sometimes I feel a sense of love or peace that is unrelated to my outer circumstance.

6. I believe that I have a unique purpose in life.

7. I find joy in serving others.

8. I try to keep a positive outlook and share goodwill with others.

9. I believe there are unseen forces that can help me in difficult times.

10. I spend some time on a regular basis to quiet my mind and stay centered.

11. I realize that difficult times are sometimes spiritual opportunities to deepen my faith.

12. I have directly experienced the power of Spirit in my life.

If you answered "false" to two or more of the above items, you may want to do some personal work in the area of spirituality.

Directions for Corrections

If you have identified a lack of spirituality as a potential roadblock to your capacity for high functioning, then create the following action plan:

1. Obtain a life coach to help you speed up your process for change.

2. Begin a daily introspection process in which you identify any psychological blocks to being more interested in deepening your spiritual realization:

a. Anger at God.

b. Excessive needs to be in control.

c. An unusual amount of anxiety.

d. Lingering trauma from early childhood religious experiences.

e. Obsessive thinking patterns in which you think life should be a certain way.

3. Prioritize the above issues and begin to systematically address them one at a time.

4. Keep a written diary of your daily progress.

5. Spend some time every day in silence and contemplation.

6. Develop a daily meditative/contemplative practice that invites Spirit into your heart.

7. Resolve your anger.

8. Spend a little time serving others.

9. Make a conscious decision to listen to your intuition and follow it! Begin small!

10. Begin each day by asking your higher power to guide and direct your life according to the divine plan.

CHAPTER 2

THE SECOND PRINCIPLE:

YOUR CAPACITY TO BELIEVE IN YOURSELF OPENS THE DOOR TO GREAT POSSIBILITIES

The mind and heart orchestrate what the body will do. When your mind is open, then anything is possible. You can limit yourself if you doubt and lose faith in your own ability. Your ultimate capacity is often tested, and when you maintain a positive self-belief in your ability to succeed, you can tap a hidden reserve. Remember our First Principle on Spirituality. Your deeper self is a reflection of the Divine and when you are aligned with the Divine, anything is possible! Never forget the God can and will use you to accomplish great things. If you can get beyond your ego, then you in conjunction with God are a powerful force.

DEVELOP AND LISTEN TO YOUR INTUITION

When you really believe in yourself, you can access a deeper intuitive knowledge of what is right and the power to manifest what you need. It is important to trust your intuition, because it is your guide and gyroscope to keep you on course. Others may doubt you, others may not support you, but when you believe in the depth of your own ability, you will make it to the other side. Your heart knows what is right for you, and when you listen to your inner voice, you can accomplish great things and survive the darkest times. This is why a consistent meditation practice is important. You are preparing and creating a solid relationship with your soul that allows for an inner peace to hear and connect with Spirit. Self-doubt, however, can undermine you and rob you of the opportunity to go deep and make that connection. When your emotions are stirred up, it is difficult to find that quiet place within.

Beware of Negative Thinking

Negative thinking, either from you or others, is deadly. It can kill your creativity and enthusiasm. It is very important to surround yourself with positive people who have an uplifting influence on you. This is especially true during difficult times, because you will need all your energy to overcome whatever obstacles confront you. Haven't you had the experience of having a great idea and sharing it with a friend who shot it down, which resulted in your losing interest in pursuing that direction? Negative influences around you are very powerful. Also, be aware of the thoughts, "I am not worthy," or "I don't deserve it." These thoughts are not your friend. Do not listen to them. Use your will to affirm positive thoughts.

Interview with Doug DeCinces

I want to share a portion of Doug DeCinces' story here, because it is so inspirational and directly speaks to this issue. As you may remember, Doug DeCinces replaced Brooks Robinson at third base for the Baltimore Orioles.

Brooks was loved by his fans and was one of the greatest players of all time. Doug was a young man, and Brooks' shoes were not easy to fill.

I asked Doug, "What was your greatest accomplishment in baseball?

"Replacing Brooks Robinson and going on to have my own career—a lot of people don't know what it's like to replace the living legend and still go out there and try to fulfill your dream. Brooks Robinson in Baltimore was—heck, he could have run for mayor and governor in the same year and won both elections. The guy was a gracious and wonderful person. Personally, we had a great relationship, but I was the guy they said was going to take his job.

"Every time I took that field to replace him, the fans in Baltimore didn't want to see me. You know, they wanted to see him. When I would go on the road, every columnist—not the beat writers, but the columnists— would come in and do this story about who's this kid thinking he can take over for the future Hall of Famer. There were some very negative things said—some positive things, but also negative things—because everybody always had an opinion. It was a better article that way.

"But more importantly, I was trying to accept that my peers, my teammates, could recognize that I could play. I had some sympathetic teammates that would come up and say, 'Hey, don't listen to that. Don't do that. Don't let these people bother you. Don't let Earl Weaver bother you. You've got to just become who you are.'

"And it would kind of wake me up, because I had put up such a fence in my own mind, to be able to get over that hurdle of not being the person that —to not let who I was replacing affect who I was trying to become.

"That's not easy. I can tell you a time where, true story, my parents brought my grandmother back to watch me play my first major league game back in Baltimore. We're playing against the Minnesota Twins in a double header. I'm not playing the first game. I started the second game. And as I'm warming up, there are 36,000 fans that day, and I was warming up and running. I'm twenty-four, twenty-five years old—you know, trying to make it. And there'd be some old Baltimore blue-collar guys yelling, 'DeCinces, you're never going to replace Brooks Robinson.'

"I'm just warming up. I'm not even in the game yet! And then they announce my name, starting third baseman, and there's that spattering of boos, just because they want to see Brooks.

"Trying not to take that personally is very difficult; and then the game's going on. Mike Cuellar is getting hit around, and there are bases loaded. And the guy hits a shot down the line. And I dive and it tips off my glove and rolls over by the tarp. And I run over, Belanger (shortstop) and I both run over and get it. By the time we get it, two runners have scored. Now fans start chanting, 'We want Brooks!'

"Well, let me tell you, Brooks wasn't going to get that ball! I mean, it was just one of those things. The stadium started picking it up: 'We want Brooks! We want Brooks!'

"And I'm standing out there going, it's a hit all the way. And sure enough, the next guy, Larry Hisle—I'll never forget him—hits a one hop shot; I mean, just a rocket. And I just cover it up. It hits me and bounces in front of me, in my chest. I go pick it up and throw to Boog Powell at first base. It's bang, bang, he's safe, and another run scores. Now I get an error for that one.

"And now the stadium is roaring. And I'm going, This is impossible! We get out of the inning. We go one, two, three, come back out, and sure enough, another ball comes to me. And now I've got this fear of making a mistake, a fearing of failure. And I'll never forget that feeling. The ball's coming, I'm thinking, Oops, don't miss it—and sure enough: error.

"Now the stadium is going again. We get out of that inning; the run doesn't score. They got five runs in the first inning. I come in. I come up to home plate. And the fans are chanting, 'We want Brooks!'

"And Gene Roof was the catcher, and he turns around and he says, 'How do you handle this?' He goes, 'Is this like this all the time you play?'

"And I said, 'Well, it's not this bad, but it can get pretty rough.'

"He says, 'All our teammates are going—our whole team's over there going, 'How the heck do you survive this?'

"Now you get that kind of thought going in your brain. You know, you get opposing guys trying to be sympathetic for you a little bit. And you see, and you start feeling—and sure enough, I strike out. I come back, and now I'm just so frustrated, you know. I've got the pressure of my grandmother here and listening to the whole stadium booing me and all that kind of stuff.

"Earl Weaver, manager of the Orioles, came up to me and he says, 'I'm going to take you out of the game,' because he was afraid that I was collapsing, and he didn't want to ruin my career. I realized right then and there that if he took me out of that game, I was never going to make it. I looked at him, and I said, 'Over my dead body!'

"I went out. I'll never forget, because Earl's a pretty gruff guy, especially in the dugout. There's not a lot of sensitivity to the man. He saw my reaction, and at that point in time I recognized I wasn't going to let these people destroy my dream.

"I mean, I got angry, and I went out and played. I'll never forget—I made every play, and every time I did, there was clapping. One time somebody threw a paper airplane. I went over and picked it up, put it in my pocket, and the stadium gives me a standing ovation. I mean, it was really bad. But my next at bat, I had an RBI single. Then my next at bat, I hit a two-run home run. I'd come up with two outs in the bottom of the ninth inning—a man on first base—and I tripled. So now I've got all four RBIs, and I'm the tying run at third base. And the stands all stood up and clapping; they were applauding me! Naturally, my mind was to show them what I thought of them. But I'll never forget—Billy Hunter was the coach who came over and he goes, 'Don't do anything that I would do.' He said, 'Just don't do it.' He was saying, 'That's how to show these people!'

"But I was still so angry. I wasn't there to reward myself at that point in time. This was my internal battle. I'd be nice to fans when I was there; it wouldn't affect who I was as a person, except when I went to play that game. I look back at that now, and one of the things that allowed me to become a clutch RBI player—and I look back at that part of my career and say, you know, I could do that; I could come up with a game on the line and not have it affect me, and be able to perform—was because of what I went through with all that. It was because—and trust me, it didn't end that day. It went on way after.

"I played eight-plus years at third base for the Orioles. I had the second most games played there. But it still would always be Brooks, no matter what I accomplished. And if I made a diving play, it was, you know, 'a Brooks Robinson play.' But that never bothered me, because I learned to get over the fact; I didn't take that personally. I took that as a compliment, because I knew what a great player and what a great person Brooks Robinson was.

"And I know that some players probably could have said, you know, 'Forget that. It's a Doug DeCinces play,' you know, or whoever you are, because they fight for their own identity. And I learned to say, 'Thank you very much,' because I looked at that always as a compliment, and not as, 'You're not recognizing who I am.' And I think mentally that allowed me to say—you know, I was very fortunate to be able to survive and be a part of what that was. The Baltimore Orioles are still a major part of who I am today."

Commentary

Wow! What a story. Talk about trial by fire. Talk about digging deep! I get anxious every time I read this story. Can you imagine being a young man of twenty-five years and having a stadium full of people booing you because you are not Brooks Robinson?

What impresses me about this story is the depth of character that is revealed. Many people would have buckled under that kind of pressure. I don't know if you can appreciate what it feels like to have 30,000 people projecting negative energy at you. I can tell you—it ain't pretty!

Doug DeCinces' ability to pull himself together and perform under those circumstances does not come from any technique. That kind of character and strength is the result of a strong inner core. That kind of inner strength and core belief is not the result of some superficial affirmation. It is the result of a solid development of self. If you do have some cracks in the foundation of your sense of self, now is the time to repair them.

It is said that we have free will, and it is our ability to choose that makes us unique as humans. Too often we hear people complaining about their circumstances and blaming others for their life's difficulties. This style of whining and complaining undermines any sense of strength and ability to conquer adversity — it is also an indication of one's character. So why is it that some people seem to rise to another level under adversity and others seem to crack? The hard truth is that it appears to be the result of an inner core—an inner sense of self that is solid, strong, and resilient. The saying, "Golf does not create character, it reveals it," speaks to this. True greatness is not the result of techniques and simple positive thinking. When all the forces of life come together to stress the very fabric of your being, to play upon your hopes and fears, and to create a path that leads either to exhilaration or despair, then and only then will the true depth of your being be revealed. Smart trash talk won't see you through—nor will hopeful thinking. When you come face-to-face with life and death—either symbolically or in reality—it is the depth of your heart and strength of your soul (that perhaps was even unknown to you until that very moment) which will lift you to a new and higher terrain of expression, and all those blessed to witness you in that moment will be uplifted and inspired by the sheer power of your being.

If there was ever a defining moment in a man's life, this was it for Doug DeCinces. His choice to stay in the game and fight for what was his—his right to play professional baseball—set the stage for a life of meaning and accomplishment. If there are angels in heaven watching over us—and I believe there are—I am sure they were thrilled when he went back onto the field!

With regards to our eight principles, we can see a few of them in action thus far in Doug's story: Belief in one's self, positive mental outlook, and heart. It is important to remember that one's inner core allows them to manifest these qualities. Mike Tyson is a good example of someone who has exceptional talent, but went off track because of tremendous internal difficulties. In one phase of his life, Mike had a very positive support system with the help of Cus D'Amato. Those around Mike all think that he lost his grounding when Cus died. Mike did not have a strong inner core of a positive sense of self, and he lost his way. I am very happy to observe that Mr. Tyson has "bounced back" and appears strong, centered, and secure. You can see all this in his stage presentation about his life. It fills my heart with joy to know that such an intelligent and talented man has made his way back into the Light.

The question naturally arises—where does this depth of being come from? Why do some people rise to the occasion and others fall? There are no simple answers to this important question. One factor is certainly the type of parenting we receive. If we are raised in a loving and stable family where our parents love and respect each other and treat us the same, then an inner core of self-worth, value, and strength is developed to help us throughout life. If we are raised with a constant barrage of, "You worthless—," "You will never amount to anything," "You will never make it," and "You are such a disappointment," you will have a lot to overcome. It is possible to overcome these early childhood messages, but it is not easy. Two individuals can have the same traumatic early childhood experiences, yet one grows up to succeed and the other fails. So childhood development is not all encompassing.

Genetic predisposition also plays a role. It is impossible to separate our psychology from our biology. We know that a family history of alcoholism creates a dangerous predilection for that same disease. Thus our genetic structure plays a part as well.

On a more esoteric level, there is a growing body of evidence and belief in the Western world that our essential nature is eternal and timeless. In the middle of 2008, Deepak Chopra was on the Bill Maher show talking about studies of children who have vivid memories of their past lives. The nature of the soul is consciousness that transcends the earthly drama of time and space. Each life has a unique expression, and consciousness continues to grow and evolve, incarnation after incarnation. So the work we do in each life is worthwhile and cumulative. We benefit from all that we do, now and in the future—we reap what we sow (law of karma).

This esoteric position is shared in many Eastern schools of thought: Buddhism, Hinduism, and the Kabbalah. Reincarnation was once a part of Christian teachings. These references were removed by the Ecumenical Council meeting of the Catholic Church in Constantinople sometime around 553 A.D., called the Council of Nicea. Some suggest that the Council members voted to strike those teachings from the Bible in order to solidify Church control.

Life can be viewed as a school for the soul to grow and evolve back into the full awareness of one's unity with Spirit. Some suggest that the soul, prior to birth, chooses a life that will provide the necessary opportunities for such growth. Life difficulties, then, become opportunities to challenge the self to learn about love, acceptance, surrender, wisdom, and our relationship with God. Each challenge becomes an opportunity to learn, grow, and become stronger.

Given this bigger perspective about the nature of the Self, our inner core is honed and developed over eternity. Our inner strength is a product of many experiences—some in this time/space continuum, and some from beyond. This is how we can move from being a constant whiner, complaining about our circumstances, to a warrior on the path of awakening.

MORE ON BELIEF IN ONESELF

I asked Doug DeCinces, "What's the greatest thing you learned from playing baseball?"

He answered, "Wow. That's a broad, broad question. You're only as good as your last at-bat.

"I knew that the confidence to go after something—that if I wanted it, I could do it—I didn't have to listen to anybody else. I was told I wasn't good enough. In high school, I was told, 'You can't play pro ball.' And then the guy who drafted me, Al Kubski, was one of the big scouts for the Orioles, and I met him, and he goes, 'I've seen you play. You can't run and you throw like a girl.'

"That was his quote to me. I was crushed. Can't run?! You know, I was a guard on the basketball team. I was a little bit thinner then. And can't throw? Man, how come I always have one of the better arms? I played shortstop in high school. The fact was he didn't like the way I did it and he felt I could be better. The next year I'm drafted by the San Diego Padres, and I didn't sign with them out of college, my first year. That was the toughest decision I ever had to make. My parents let me make it, too."

I asked, "Why did you choose not to sign with them?"

"They wouldn't guarantee my education. I was a fifth-round pick, and they wouldn't guarantee my education? Back then, that was when the Padres had no money. Ray Kroc and McDonald's hadn't bought them yet. And I just refused it. I had scholarship offers and places I could have gone. I had a successful first year of college. I had scholarship offers out of high school. And I said, 'If I'm good enough, I'm going to get drafted again.' Well, guess who drafted me the next summer? That same guy that said I couldn't run and I threw like a girl!

"And I remember seeing him when I got traded out here to the Angels, and he'd come to the game, and we'd sit and talk. And he goes, 'You know, you always had the mental capability of not being satisfied.' Maybe that's something I learned out of it. Never be satisfied, because there's always an opportunity to be better. I learned that from Brooks Robinson. Brooks Robinson, arguably the greatest fielding third baseman in the history of the game—he would take forty ground balls every single day. Okay, now, I'm a rookie, and I'm supposed to be the guy replacing this guy. Well, if he's taking forty, how am I going to replace him taking forty? I'd take sixty there, sixty at short, sixty at second. I'd wear out the coaches every single day, because it was that type of approach that was going to allow me to be successful. So maybe that's what I learned the most.

"And the other thing is: don't take yourself too seriously, because there's always somebody who's going to humble you in a hurry. That's why I said you're only as good as your last at-bat. You hit a grand slam? Hey, great. Come back up — game's on the line — you strike out — you lose. Who cares what you did with the grand slam? The fact is you didn't win the game."

Commentary

I think that this part of Doug DeCinces' story is invaluable for kids today. There are always people who will say, "You aren't good enough." If you let other people define you, you are throwing away your potential. You have to believe in yourself. Read the sections on Dick Fosbury. The Eastern European coaches told him he could not win with his high jump style. They all told him to stop doing it. Where would he be today if he had listened to them? Also, read the sections on Lee Brandon. She had her arm severed in an accident and the doctors wanted to amputate it. They said she would never be able to use it. Not so—she became the Women's World Long Drive Champion with two arms. After years of hard work, determination, and self-belief, she rehabilitated her damaged arm.

When I was in high school, I was pretty lost. I went to UCLA and had a full battery of aptitude and psychological tests to help me figure out what I should do in life. After twenty hours of testing and interviewing, the "experts" told me I would never make it in higher education. They recommended that I become a printer, because I showed some interest in graphic arts. Where in the world would I be if I had listened to them? I certainly would not have a Ph.D., have written an LA Times best-selling book (*Sacred Healing: Integrating Spirituality with Psychotherapy*), and I would certainly not be writing this book right now!

Doug's advice is also great. Work hard to achieve your goals. You can't just sit back and expect to be successful. Sometimes it takes a lot more work to do well than we think. I was shocked when I went to college at UCSB. I had to work twice as hard as I did in high school. But once I realized that is what it took, I was fine. I adjusted and put out the effort.

Dick Fosbury's story also has elements regarding this issue of self-belief. Dick and I were talking about how others viewed his technique and the support he received from his coaches. I commented, "When you're describing your experiences with the coaches, on the one hand, they sound like they were supportive of you, but they were still trying to get you to do something more conventional."

Dick replied, "Yeah, always, of course. That's what you know. When you're a coach, that's what you know. That's what you're taught, and so, of course. However, my coaches were always very supportive and helped me to do the best that I could. And when I got to the Olympics and began to meet coaches from other countries—that's where I received the most criticism. The coaches, the Russians and the Germans, were very technique-oriented, and they knew the techniques that the world record holder used. They'd all studied the films, and they had coached all their athletes to do what Brumel did. And so all of them had very similar approaches—very mechanical, though. And when I met them, they were not just critical, but they believed it was a fact that I would never win. And you know, I listened to them, but I just shrugged my shoulders and said, "Well, you know, all I can do is what I can do. I mean, I have my techniques. That's what I brought to this game, and let's go play the game."

I commented, "I'm sure you're aware that some people would have started to doubt themselves at that point."

Dick said, "You know, that's a good point. On the other hand, I was on a hot streak. I had an excellent year, and I'd improved my best by four inches, which is one of those exceptional years. Normal physical growth—a high jumper ought to improve by three inches a year, but I was having an exceptional year and I had made the Olympic team. I was competing at the highest level, so I had a lot of stuff to keep my confidence, to build my confidence. I was not that confident in my abilities that I would ever brag about what I was doing, but I kept it to myself. You know, I always had self-doubt, but I had no experience with foreign coaches and so I didn't put any stock into it, because I didn't know. I just didn't know those guys and whether they knew something I didn't know, whether they're telling the truth, or what?

"So I think part of it, once again, is that the nature of that individual event, where you have to be independent—you do learn to rely on your coach, but when you're down on the field, it's you and nobody else. And so what you're pointing out to me is absolutely correct. I understand what you're saying, and yet at the same time, if you have self-doubts when you're down on the stadium in front of 80,000 people, you're probably not going to succeed. And so I had learned—I had developed an ability to block things out, all of the external events that were going on; block out what I couldn't use and incorporate what I could use, which is the positive attention that I was receiving, the cheering, and just the mere attention itself. I always used that to psych myself up—raise my level of intensity, raise my adrenaline, but control it."

COMMENTARY

Dick Fosbury is a great example of someone who had the good fortune to have a solid psychological foundation and an inner strength to trust himself and allow his development to unfold. He worked hard and had good supporting coaches, and he always came back to his own sense of what was right for him. He developed tools on his own—visualization, a feeling approach to sports, focusing, and an openness to forces greater than himself (refer back to the first chapter on spirituality), all of which are now basics for sport psychology. His moment of excellence took his life to a new height— physically, psychologically, and spiritually—and has resulted in a life filled with meaning and service to others.

Jim Brown mentioned in his interview the need to understand who you are and respect that. Here are some thoughts about that from Jim Brown.

JIM BROWN ON INDIVIDUAL GIFTS

"Well, let me give you a well-rounded approach to any athletic success. First of all, each one of us has something from birth—genetics. And each one of us is a separate individual. So it means that normal teaching applies in general, but an individual that wants to really excel has to really understand what his gifts are—his natural physical gifts. You have to start with that.

"Take myself, for example. I was a combination kind of a person. I was big, but I had really fine coordination. I had good balance; I had good quickness and good speed and good strength. So I had a good combination. Now that works a certain way in basketball, it works a certain way in track and field; it works a certain way in football and lacrosse. So I couldn't approach each game—each sport—doing the same thing.

"So you learn how to orchestrate your physicality. For example, I had very thick thighs. And people said, 'Oh, you get real flexible when you play football and you do all this stretching,' but I really didn't want to stretch them out. I wanted the size and the bulk and the compactness of my thighs along with my body to create a force. And it worked really well for football. It isn't great for track when you're going to be a high jumper, so my high jump was limited because I had to rely mainly on my spring, and I couldn't really kick. My hamstrings wouldn't allow me to kick as high as one should be able to do it, so I was a decent high jumper, just using force—I mean, mere force of my legs. So to make a long story short, we each have something physically that we're endowed with."

BUCK RODGERS ON SELF-BELIEF

I was asking Buck about coaches and his experience with good coaches. Our discussion led to this material. Buck had the inner strength and clarity to follow his own wisdom and do what he felt was right for him, even when his coaches had other ideas.

"Well, I think that you pick a little bit out of every coach's repertoire. I was originally with the Detroit system, and Mickey Cochran was my catching coach. And Mickey Cochran was one of the all-time Hall of Famers, but he was a small man. So he had a different way of catching. So this larger catcher, bigger catcher, and not as famous, never did make the Major League—he saw that I was getting very frustrated, and so he said, 'Rodgers, come out at 8:00 in the morning, meet me at Cobb field, we're going to go do some things. Coach Cochran is a very good catcher, but he's a small man. You and I are big guys, we can do this, but we have to do it this way.' Al Lakeman was his name, and I think he was very instrumental in my mentally becoming a catcher—a Major League catcher.

"There's certain things you have to let go in one ear and out the other. I was a switch-hitter. In Detroit, some of the guys wanted me to hit all right-handed; I was a better right-handed hitter. A year or so later, I had a manager that wanted me to hit all left-handed, the opposite way. I never changed; I was steadfast in my belief that I could be a switch-hitter. Sometimes you have to know more than your coach! I think that was a very important part of my career—that I didn't do what these coaches wanted me to do. I thought switch-hitting was a definite way for me to get to the Major Leagues. That's why I worked on it. I thought I was good enough to do that. I knew I was better one side than the other. But other times, it would switch back and forth from week to week and month to month—but I knew, overall, that was my best way to get to the Major Leagues."

COMMENTARY

We all have God-given talents. We need to realize and play to those strengths. If you are a turtle, you are not going to fly! Michael Phelps, the fantastic 2008 Olympic gold medal winner in swimming was asked in an interview about his strategy. He replied, "I use the best tools I have, and my dolphin kick is one of my strengths." He knew his talents and capitalized on them.

One of the most common errors I see in golf instruction is the "one size fits all" approach. Often the less talented instructors will give the same advice to every student. It does not matter how old they are, the shape their body is in, or their level of talent. They use the video equipment to show the perfect swing and attempt to get the student to become that. Let's face it—you don't need the "perfect" swing to make a lot of money. There are guys on the Champions Tour making a lot of money with a swing that looks so bad I don't know how they even make it as a professional golfer. But they do, and they have perfected their way of doing something based upon their body. They can repeat the same swing and have consistency. They are not trying to be someone else. Know who you are, and play to your strengths!

It is amazing how many times we hear from great athletes that someone tried to change their way of competing or just told them that they would never be able to compete. Where would Dick Fosbury be if the Russian and European Olympic coaches had psychologically affected him? Buck's story is a lesson to us all: "to thine own self be true." This is an ancient message that never becomes outdated. In every aspect of your life, you need to honor yourself. Life will test you; life will tempt you to give yourself away with the promise that if you follow someone else's advice, you will be more successful. Life is often a test to challenge your authenticity, to discover if you have the courage to stand up and be. It takes courage and a strong will to hold your ground, plant your flag, and set your boundaries.

What do you think makes great comics so funny? People like Jerry Seinfeld and Chris Rock have the courage to stand up and be themselves.

Larry Liberty, who you probably never heard of, is an independent corporate consultant. We met on the golf course, became friends, and eventually worked together. He was a great mentor for me in my corporate training. I was amazed at how authentic he was in a group of people. He said what was on his mind and got away with it. In fact, he got paid a lot of money to do so. I was shocked at how honest he was and the things he would say to people. He inspired me to take more chances and speak up.

Jim Brown offers some profound information in his first breath: "Know who you are!" In many sports, coaches and parents take a cookie-cutter approach and treat everyone the same. This may have worked well for creating the Model T Ford, but it does not work if your goal is to create champions.

Jim Brown is a profound thinker and has a depth of psychological wisdom. When you apply this to your physicality, then you have another advantage. If your natural shot is to draw the ball, then it is best to rely on that shot. If your body and swing want to fade it, but you resist that and want to hit a draw, then you may be fighting against your natural ability and natural style.

Shakespeare knew this. "To thine own self be true." Therefore, some of the initial work needs to be in understanding who you are and what you have to work with.

The natural question arises, "How do I know who I am?" This question is answered through honest self-evaluation and introspection. It is easy, and unfortunately all too common, to inflate one's sense of self. People like to brag or boast that they are more successful than they really are. People lie about how much money they make, give themselves four-foot putts all day long, and then declare they shot at seventy-eight. If you really want to know who you are, take an honest look at what you have done and what you can do. Now, potential is not the same as capacity. Potential is what you might be able to do, and capacity is what you can actually do. It is important to understand both and to honestly acknowledge what your current capacity is—all the while striving to reach your potential.

Introspection is also a key tool in understanding your true self. The mind is full of doubt, fear, and limitations that keep you from being your best. Introspection can allow you to clearly see your beliefs and attitudes that create limitations and learn to dis-identify with those thoughts and beliefs. Do not define yourself by the passing thoughts from your mind. The best athletes are able to sustain a very positive mind state and reinforce that belief throughout life. However, it is essential to realize that self-confidence is related to self-knowledge! You can maintain a strong positive belief in yourself when you really know who you are and realize that you have a strong foundation based upon real tangible assets and accomplishments.

DOUG DeCINCES AND STEROIDS

The following discussion about the impact of steroids on baseball is very interesting. It relates to several areas of our discussion: belief in yourself, spiritual awareness, individuation, and emotional maturity. I include it now, because anyone who chooses to use steroids has some doubt about his or her ability to fully compete and be successful based solely upon his or her God-given talent. We pay a price when we try to cut corners and find an edge. It can be through performance-enhancing drugs or shady business practices. The results can be the same. Eventually the truth comes out, and we lose something. All along the way we have lost our integrity, which creates a gap in the heart and a wound to the soul. Here is what Doug had to say about steroid use and my comments. I asked, "What do you think about the steroid problem in baseball?"

INTERVIEW

"I think if you're talking about the mental approach, obviously the mental approach is that somebody's taking steroids because it makes them physically stronger and play better. And they're not thinking about tomorrow; they're thinking about today. I think until Major League Baseball and everybody stepped up and said, 'Hey, this is illegal,' I don't think you can really condemn those guys beforehand. But frankly, I don't think Rafael Palmeiro should go to the Hall of Fame. He's accomplished a lot, but he accomplished it on illegal drugs that he knew he shouldn't have been taking. I may be a little outspoken about that, but guys who took steroids, I mean, guys are hitting … Barry Bonds hitting seventy-plus home runs a year. I said, 'You know, that's physically impossible.' And yet they're just blowing through record books after record, and just making a mockery of all the guys that played before who didn't do that. I hit 240 in my career. Well, if I would have taken steroids, I can tell you I hit 240 balls to the warning track that probably would go out if I were taking steroids.

"So, where does that put me in the—or all my other peers that went out and played without it? I played with some guys I knew that were taking it, and it totally changed their physical abilities, 100 percent. So is that the right thing to do? I know when my son was in the Minor Leagues; we had numerous conversations because he said, 'Dad, how am I supposed to compete? If I don't take it, how am I supposed to compete?'

"And I said, 'You compete on what God gave you. And if you can't do it on that, then you need to do something else!'

"Now, I'll be the first to tell you that I drank coffees, and, you know, I did things that help you get up. That's a long season and stuff like that. But I never took any steroids or anything like that. Heck, when I was going through there, there was a huge cocaine problem. I was the head of the Players' Association at that time. We're trying to take care of the Willie Wilsons and all the guys, the Norrises and guys like that who got busted for it all the time. It was more of a cocaine problem in the big leagues than steroids. And now you look at this. You see players this year and the last three years —you look at them — and how did they get that good? But the guys are sitting there, and they're going, 'Do I have a choice? I take them so I can stay in the big leagues and make my money and fulfill my dream. But if I don't take them, that general manager is going to send me back down, because he's going to bring up a kid that is taking them.'

"So I think baseball is more at error than the players. I mean, it's a pressure-driven job, to go out and compete on 161, 162 games a year and to go against the greatest in the world, and somebody's saying, 'Hey, look at the results I get from taking this'—oh my gosh. Guys aren't going think to—you know—their mindset is to take it. 'Okay, let's go take it.'

"But then there are others' mindsets that say, 'Hey, that's not the right way to do it.' And now how do they compete against the guys that are cheating? I mean, you look at Ivan Rodriguez this year [2006]. He's not even the same person that's been an All-Star every year as a catcher [13 years on All-Star team]. You look at— I'm just going to be glancing around, but, how do guys in their late forties throw ninety-plus miles an hour? Think they're doing that all by themselves? I don't think so. You know, I would say Nolan Ryan was one of those guys that was really unique. But he had a unique body. But he wasn't all of a sudden twenty-five pounds heavier and—you know, looking all different. I look at that thing that happened with Roger Clemens and Piazza. How do you go off like that? Steroids do some things to your brains and stuff like that, too.

"That's just kind of the way I look at it. I think it's wrong. And I think that Palmeiro, of all guys this year—you stand in front of Congress and point your finger at them, and then you go out and take it? And look at Sammy Sosa this year. He's not taking steroids. You look at him, and he's shrunk down enormously and his bat's way back here. It's not out in front, hitting home runs anymore. It's back here. He can't catch up to the ball. There's a marked physical difference in their abilities, your quick twitch muscles and all those things that require you to hit a fastball further or to throw a ball harder. You see a lot of pitchers today, they all of a sudden—they were throwing ninety-three. All those guys that are in the Hall of Fame back there —a lot of pitchers cut balls, use pine tar, use spit, use what else, you know? That's kind of—how do you say it's cheating? It is cheating. It's part of the game, but it's cheating, and if you can get away with it, I guess they'd do it. It's like the guy that used corked bats. If you can get away with it, you do it. But, you know, I remember using a corked bat against Gaylord Perry in a game. It was a joke how much he was cheating on the mound. And so I borrowed somebody's bat on my team, and I went up there—hit a double in right center. I'm standing on second base going, 'Nobody pick up that bat. Oh my gosh.' I was scared to death, you know, scared to death. And I never, ever used a cork bat. I used it one time, one at-bat, and got a double, and I don't think it would have made a difference."

COMMENTARY

Steroids use in baseball is a rather complex economic, ethical, and spiritual issue. I believe it is unfair to only blame the individual players without taking into account the larger organization and cultural factors. Individual players have tacitly been given permission by baseball to use drugs. At first, it was individuals who made the choice; but once the organization looked the other way, the culture became corrupted. Individual players were trying to make a living and compete. They took the drug to remain competitive. That is the economic reality. Some may argue that if they wanted to remain in the majors, they had to do it.

However, there are also ethical issues. Does one allow himself or herself to become corrupt because of financial gain and worldly success? In the American culture, the answer is often yes! Our culture is built around fame, power, and fortune. We often place money above anything else—especially in sports and the business world. Does it matter that historic records were being broken because players had a physical advantage from drug enhancement? If the drug use was openly acknowledged, then the answer might be no. But it becomes a much different ethical matter when players lie about the truth and still claim the victories.

Is there much difference here between lying about using performance enhancing drugs in sports and lying about the finances of a business? How about lying about the nature of low-interest loans? How about lying about investment programs that rob people of billions of dollars? All this is based in greed—the desire to get more at any cost. The United States has paid a huge price for this type of ethic.

With regards to surviving during very difficult times, does it matter how we get there? Are we only concerned about performance, about success, and about winning, or are we also interested in the process of victory and what that process does for the development of the individual? The intent of this book is to look at the deeper character aspects among great athletes to see what we can learn about life, the human will, and the human spirit. This book is not a cookbook about how to win and make a lot of money. It is about finding your way through difficult times without losing your soul.

Peak performance has magical moments, like when Dick Fosbury is being lifted over the bar to win an Olympic gold medal. Those who believe in a spiritual reality believe that there is a relationship between the human will, the human spirit, and God. What resides in one's heart is important. A pure heart can attract many wonderful and wondrous things. When a person takes a drug, then something is lost. The experience becomes, at best, a peak at a potential or possibility, but it does not become an integrated part of one's being. What is lost is the real growth of human consciousness and human ability to move to the next level. Once you take away the drug, then you strip away the ability to actually perform at that level.

On might argue that life is an experience to learn something more about who we really are, not just to make a lot of money and gain power and prestige. This learning process is most profound when we draw upon our natural inner resources that transcend our human condition and lift us to a high realm—a realm that clears the mind, opens the heart, and touches the soul. Sports have the ability to do this. The movie The Natural did such a thing. Real victory in the sports world inspires us all to greater hopes and greater accomplishments.

The spiritual loss with drug use in sports is that our children learn the wrong message. They learn that wining at any cost is more important than honesty, integrity, and the evolution of the human will. They become robbed of the deeper meaning of life and are sold a Madison Avenue marketing version of life's meaning and purpose. While it is exciting to see a ball hit 400 yards and pitchers throwing in the nineties, baseball is about more than that—all sports are. The magic of peak performance is lost when success is only attributed to chemical means. The magic of life is also lost when we turn to drugs and alcohol when life becomes too stressful. Life will test us, and with the right methods, we can find the strength to overcome all adversity. While chemicals may help soften the pain and dull the senses, they do not provide a means for mastery.

The use of marijuana is a relevant issue here, especially as a way to cope with stress. While medical marijuana may have its place, daily use for stress release has its problems. During my many years in clinical practice as a psychologist, I saw people with the complaint that their lives did not seem to be going anywhere. These individuals were kind and loving and just did not seem to have the drive to accomplish what they desired. These people were getting stoned every day! Pain, frustration, and discomfort can be a great motivator for change. If you artificially take away the pain, all life is good. The saying "no pain, no gain" may have some relevance here.

While the ethical discussion might seem beyond the scope of this book, I believe it is important, because my goal is to do more than just provide a road-map for success. While honesty and integrity may not be necessary for peak performance—and in fact, it appears they are not—these qualities do matter in higher ethical realms. Sports provide a model for young people on how to live. Professional sports are just a game. How one relates to friends, spouses, business partners, etc. Is not a game. If the message becomes "win at any cost," then the human spirit takes a hit. We lose trust and respect for each other and damage our ability to relate as a society. How we play the game is as important as whether or not we win! Golf is probably the one sport that maintains its commitment to this high ethical and moral standard. It is the only sport where a player will call a penalty upon himself. The bottom line is that you do not have faith in yourself to come out the other side if you look to external, artificial supports to get you there. Don't be seduced by the promise of "success" if you have to cheat, lie, or steal. Learn to develop the trust and faith in your inner core—your true self—and you will become stronger and enhance the essential values that mark a victorious life: integrity, honesty, perseverance, and faith.

SELF-ANALYSIS—SELF-BELIEF

Answer the following questions: True or False

1. When I fall short of my own expectations, I forgive myself.

2. I regard my father with great esteem.

3. I choose friends who respect me.

4. I choose friends who are sensitive.

5. I value my contributions to the world.

6. I respect my mother.

7. I respect my friends and loved ones.

8. I do not need to be perfect in everything I do.

9. I do not allow other people to walk all over me.

If you answered "false" to two or more of the above items, you may need to do some personal work in the area of self-belief.

DIRECTIONS FOR CORRECTIONS

If you have identified self-belief as a potential roadblock to your capacity for high functioning, then create the following action plan:

1. Obtain a life coach to help you speed up your process for change.

2. Begin a daily introspection process in which you identify any psychological blocks that limit your self-belief:

   a. Any childhood messages that you were "not good enough."

   b. Any sense of shame.

   c. Any doubt about your capacity to be successful.

   d. Any underlying depression that creates negative self-talk.

   e. Rigid childhood conditioning that prevents you from setting appropriate limits and boundaries with others.

3. Prioritize the above issues and begin to systematically address them one at a time.

4. Keep a written diary of your daily progress.

5. Create a positive affirmation regarding your worth and value.

6. Develop a daily meditative/contemplative practice that assesses your willingness to change.

7. Make a conscious decision to improve any part of your life that does not represent how you want to be.

8. Begin each day by asking your higher power to guide and direct your life so you can be the best you can be.

CHAPTER 3

THE THIRD PRINCIPLE:

POSITIVE MIND STATE

IF YOU CAN MAINTAIN A POSITIVE STATE OF MIND, YOU WILL EXPONENTIALLY INCREASE THE PROBABILITY OF ACHIEVING YOUR GOALS

A positive mental outlook is essential for success and victory. A positive mental approach creates a strong flow of energy and dynamic willpower. Negative thinking deflates your ability to act, persevere under pressure, and remain psychologically and physically healthy. We know from watching sports that self-confidence is a magnet that draws success. We see it on the golf course when a player is putting well and everything seems to drop. Players report, "I knew it was going in!" Self-confidence and a positive mental state are interconnected.

A fundamental esoteric principle is, "Energy follows thought." It therefore follows that the body cannot achieve what the mind conceives to be impossible! The ability to maintain a positive mental outlook will open doors to new possibilities.

Jim Brown had some important things to say about developing self-confidence and keeping the mind strong.

JIM BROWN

"You need repetition and hard work. Now, there are two things that hard work gives you. One is, it familiarizes you with everything, it gets you in great condition, it prepares you, you know, mentally and physically to approach your profession. The other thing that it really gives you is confidence, which is about the mind. If you know you haven't worked hard enough and prepared yourself properly—now you're going on what you have naturally. But a lot of times, if things don't go right, psychologically you lose ground because you know you haven't prepared the way you should.

"If you know you're in total shape and you've prepared in every way and something goes wrong, you can bounce back from it much easier. You don't necessarily lose confidence; you can just stick in there because you know you have prepared yourself, and you can max it. That's very important. It's hard to get around.

"A great talent that cheats on hard work and preparation is never going to be a strong psychological force. You just can't do it, because you tell yourself the truth—you can bullshit your opponent. You can deal with a facade, but it's a very hollow facade, because you know that you have not properly prepared."

COMMENTARY

Mr. Brown's comments about preparation address two levels. One level is more physical and mechanical—preparation gives you more ability to function under pressure and successfully repeat an action time and time again. One develops consistency, because the skills developed through practice become integrated into the body memory.

The other level is much deeper; it is the psychological level. One of the most striking things about Jim Brown is his intensity. His energy is, in part, due to his fierce commitment to honesty. He does not like B.S.! He is giving some profound advice regarding the building blocks for self-esteem, self-confidence, and a strong mental outlook. It is easy to pretend and create a facade. However, anyone with a degree of awareness can see through this mask. Moreover, this facade has no depth; it has no substance and will not stand up to the pressure of competition or adversity. If you know who you are, what you have accomplished, and the extent to which you have prepared, then it is possible to really trust yourself to come through when it counts. True greatness is typically measured by the ability to respond to adversity. It is very difficult to respond with greatness when your inner foundation is weak from lack of practice, lack of preparation, and lack of self-knowledge. Therefore, real self-confidence generates a positive mental outlook, because it is built upon a foundation of work and personal development—physically, spiritually, and psychologically.

This relationship between preparation and the ability to maintain a positive state of mind—especially during times of crisis—is paramount. When crisis hits, you will be thrown into an established coping style. If you have not prepared yourself by daily practice to have a solid, consistent foundation comprised of peace of mind, trust in the universe to support you, and a positive belief in your own capacity to manifest what you need, you will probably be thrown into an emotional reaction of fear, anger, doubt, and confusion. When a crisis hits, it is not the best time to begin learning good coping skills. Hopefully you have developed a lifestyle and a solid foundation of these core principles that you can put into action when you most need them. Just like health care, prevention is the best form of treatment.

INTERVIEW WITH DIEGO CORRALES

It is worth noting what Diego Corrales had to say about his work ethic:

"The one thing that I really take pride in is how I work. I work, and I know I work harder than, I'd say, at least 90 percent of the boxing community right now. And I'd say I could maybe see one, two people working as hard or harder. It's very hard to work at the way I work every day, at the pace I work every day. It's hard to do that. But I just somehow wake up every day looking to do it again."

THE POWER OF THOUGHT

The ability to maintain a positive mental outlook is essential for success. It is especially critical during challenging times, because the collective field around you is negative, confused, and in emotional turmoil; fear is running amok among the majority, and a doom-and-gloom mentality can be contagious. It is very important to have a solid inner core that is based upon sound principles that allow you to keep a positive outlook and see through the veil of darkness to the light at the end of the tunnel.

A fundamental esoteric principle is, "Energy follows thought." Therefore, what begins in the mind becomes energy and eventually is expressed through action and behavior. The body cannot achieve what the mind conceives to be impossible!

Because thought is energy—and we are all, at the most essential level, energy—we pick up or absorb these energy fields and become influenced by them. Individuals who are very aware and sensitive to subtle impressions actually feel this happening. It is very important, then, to surround yourself with positive people and influences in order to maintain confidence and a positive state of mind. Negative people can rob you of your personal power and undermine your confidence to accomplish great things. Paramahansa Yogananda has a great saying, "Environment is stronger than will power."

Sankhya yoga philosophy, an Eastern perspective on creation, describes everything in creation, including thought, as subtle vibrations that emanate from the Divine. The level or quality of vibrations results in the appearance of physical, material reality. Sankhya philosophy suggests that creation is a more condensed form of the Divine Spirit. As Spirit descends into matter, it does so because of changes in vibration from lighter to denser states. While this may seem difficult to understand or believe, a common example from ordinary life may help. Let's consider water in its various forms. As you know, frozen water becomes a solid in the form of ice. When we heat it up—speed up its molecular activity—it returns to a liquid and eventually disappears as a gas. With condensation, it changes vibration, solidifies, and returns to a liquid state. One way to think about this is as the vibration changes, so does its appearance in physical, material reality.

It is important to realize that what you think does make a difference. Your state of mind affects you and those around you. In fact, there have been some interesting studies done in Japan by Dr. Masaru Emoto with thought and water crystals. Different thoughts like love and hate were projected at water, and then the frozen water crystals were observed under a microscope. The results are dramatic. The more elevated thoughts resulted in beautiful and symmetric shapes as opposed to the more negative thought forms that created grotesque forms! Do an Internet search on "emoto," and you will see the images.

You will see from the pictures that positive thoughts create beautiful, symmetrical patterns, and negative thoughts are rather ugly and grotesque. This is also true with the thought forms associated with people, such as the difference between Hitler and Mother Teresa.

It is essential to remember that humans are made of a large percentage of water. Therefore, how you think directly determines your biological composition at a cellular level. Positive mental states are very powerful in creating health and wellness. We know that stress is a major factor in disease. Given our current world economic, security, and political tensions, there is plenty of stress to go around. In order to maintain your mental and physical well being, you need to take positive, proactive measures. It is impossible to function at your best, which is imperative during these difficult times, when you are physically ill. Major loss of any kind ranks high on the stress scale. If you get physically ill during times of crisis, it becomes much more difficult to cope. The various principles offered here provide a path and a method for peace of mind and coping that will help you lower your stress level, make good decisions, and stay healthy when life gets really tough.

Please remember our discussion in the chapter on spirituality. In this chapter I share my conversation with Jim Brown regarding spiritual forces, the mind and our ability to positively influence others. It is very important to acknowledge this aspect of our being, and Jim Brown has a lot to say about this. In fact, he has a strong mystical awareness that has allowed him to work with gangs and help many find a better life. He talks about learning to live in truth and opening to a different reality. He is so respected for his physical accomplishments in sports that it is important to recognize his deeper spiritual nature as well.

THE HIGHER MIND

Any discussion on the power of thought would not be complete without including the impact of visualization and attachments. The worldly, conventional view of positive thinking is to believe in a particular positive outcome—be positive that you will get that job, find a particular house, meet the soul mate of your dreams, etc. All of these outcomes are based upon preconceived ideas of what would be good and personally fulfilling. The recent promotion of The Secret has some of these elements, because it is promoted as a way to get what you want through the power of your intent—i.e., positive mental state. Visualization techniques are used to create strong mental imagery to picture and focus on personal desires. The hope and promise is that the constant inner vigil with the specific visualization will lead to the manifestation of the desired goal—you get what you want!

While it is true that you can directly influence and facilitate your reality within the scope of your karma, you may not be creating the highest possible result for yourself. You may be limiting yourself through your ideas of what is best for you. Your hopes and dreams may be less than what the Divine has in store for you. Of course, if you do have strong desires, it is good to fulfill them so you can move on. However, if you can move to a higher state where you can let go of your attachment to your desire and trust in the abundance of the Divine, you might get more that you thought possible. The idea is to get yourself out of the way and let God bring to you what you need. "Seek ye first the kingdom of God, and all things shall be added unto you." Therefore, if you can hold a positive mental state that affirms, "God will provide," you can be supported through the trials and tribulations of physical, psychological, and economic crises.

Swami Satchidananda was a great spiritual teacher and enlightened being who founded the Integral Yoga Society. I was blessed to have him as a friend when he was alive. He was on my Board of Directors for Projects for Planetary Peace when we were creating Citizen Diplomacy missions with the Soviet Union. He accompanied us on a major trip with eighty other people in the 1980s. During an overnight train trip from Finland to Leningrad (St. Petersburg), he shared with me his story of renunciation:

SWAMI SATCHIDANANDA

"I was fifteen years old and decided to turn my life over to God. I said to God, 'You will have to feed me. I will not ask for food from anyone. I will only take water from a public fountain.'

"I began to walk and did not have a single penny to my name. I did not have a pocket to put it in, even if I had a penny. I was only wearing my doti. I walked and walked, day after day after day. Five days went by, I was very hungry. I was sitting in a train station, and the ticket agent came over to me and asked, 'Swamiji, do you want to go to Rishikesh?'

"I was not a swami, but I said, 'All right.' He gave me the ticket.

"I was sitting there on the platform for a few hours, and someone came over and gave me a piece of fruit. Soon another person gave me another piece of fruit. Shortly I had so much food I had to give it away. I had more than I could eat. This is how it works. Ask for nothing and God will give you everything you need."

Swami Satchidanada had millions of dollars at his command as the head of the Integral Yoga Society. He was a living example of his teachings.

Swamiji told me this story late in the evening in his cabin. He and

I were the only ones present, and I was especially attentive to his state of consciousness. I did my best to attune to his vibration. Upon my return back home, I went out to dinner the first evening. I was alone at a local restaurant in Nevada City, California. Upon completion, I asked the waitress for the bill. She informed me that someone had already paid it for me.

Cracks in the Mind
José Torres

José Torres and I were talking about the mental side of boxing, and he shared some thoughts about a match he had with Willie Pastrano. He regarded Willie as one of his best friends:

"I can remember my friend, Willie Pastrano. When I hit him a couple of times, he changed in the first round — I noticed that change. He became a little discouraged when he could not do his thing. Then in the sixth round, I hit him with a body punch; he went down and was in pain. I knew that he was in pain and I walked to my neutral corner knowing that was the beginning of the end— even though in the first round I knew it. I controlled the fight. I don't think that Willie Pastrano won a minute of that fight with me. There was not a round or a minute when I wasn't on top of him. And mentally and psychologically, when you are controlling a fight, and you know that you are controlling a fight, you don't get tired. You only get tired if the other guy's hitting you once in a while, because when you are in top physical condition—which most fighters are—the tiredness is more psychological; it's fear. Your mind is always looking for an excuse."

Commentary

Mr. Torres casually drops a huge bomb here—"your mind is always looking for an excuse." There have been thousands of pages written on this subject of the mind; just check out the Buddhist and Vedanta literature. This simple thought, "your mind," suggests that there is a difference between who you are and what your mind has to say. Many people really think they are just the mind.

All meditation traditions are designed to help the student differentiate the true Self from the mind. Hours, years, even lifetimes are spent in observing the breath and developing the capacity to distinguish between the contents of the mind and the real Self or soul. The mind says, "I am tired, I want to quit." The degree to which you are aligned with the Self determines whether or not you will listen to that complaint. A realized Self can have more influence to direct the will than the mind. A strong Self directs the will and moves past the limitations of the mind. A strong will, directed by the Self, will result in a calm and focused mind that remains directed on the object of concentration. When the will is weak, the mind bounces around and jumps all over the place.

A weak mind will undermine any great potential. A weak-minded individual will undermine the effectiveness of a group. It is easy to be negative, create doubt, and stop the progression into new territory. Fear is usually the underlying force. This negative fear-based tactic is the most common strategy in today's political arena. "Don't vote for lying, cheating …." Attack, belittle, and demean those who disagree with you. People believe what they hear and get all emotionally worked up and terrified, even in the lack of tangible proof and facts. If you do not have a strong inner core, you can more easily be influenced by other's thoughts and opinions.

The central point here is that the deeper Self should be the guiding force for action. However, when one learns how to develop the higher mind—a mind that is a function of the soul—then a clearer discriminative capacity is developed. This higher mind, known as Buddhi in Sankhya yoga philosophy, is the discriminative intellect that is wiser and clearer. An essential part of any training for success is the development of a strong, clear mind that is focused upon the chosen goal.

It is imperative that during difficult and uncertain times you do not become influenced by and reactive to the collective fear. This fear may come from your immediate family if you have been diagnosed with a terminal illness. It may come from those around you in your business when a financial crisis hits. Wherever it comes from, you will be on more solid ground if you can keep a clear head and be guided by a deeper compass. If you stay on course and follow the direction that comes from your higher self and intuitive wisdom, you will be all right.

ON FEAR

Any discussion about the mind and positive thinking must include a discussion about fear, because the mind creates fear. There are different sources which can create fear—i.e., loss, pain, rejection, failure, etc. Let's hear what these great athletes have to say about fear.

DOUG DECINCES ON FEAR

Doug DeCinces said, "I think one of the big things that probably changes athletes—in crucial situations or not—is the fear of failure. I always felt that the fear of failure could reach up and grab you more than anything else, to turn you from being successful to a failure in clutch situations. I think every athlete—and I don't care if you're the greatest clutch player in the world— can't sit here and say that isn't something that doesn't enter your mind. You're laying awake at night, going to a World Series game the next day, and thinking, 'God, I've got to do good. I hope I don't …' The negative thoughts start falling into you. It's like when you're in a slump, and you go, 'God, I just feel terrible. I can't … I'm not seeing the ball. I'm not …' Every one of those things are negative thoughts and allow you to just twirl down lower and lower, versus clearing the mind and having confidence that you have the ability to compete."

I asked him, "Did you have a way of dealing with that fear of failure?"

"I would go from that to using the aggressively anger approach—anger, but aggressive. 'You're challenging me, and I'm going to beat you, and there's not going to be any if's, and's, or but's about this.' When you're in that mindset in that key situation, it goes back to maybe my Brooks Robinson stuff—I knew that I had all my attention on what I was trying to do.

"And I'll tell you; there were times when a pitcher would knock me down, throw a ball at my head. Trust me, I got right back up and said, 'You want to hit me, you can throw this one inside, because I'm going to hit this outside pitch right back up the middle.'

"Yeah. My goal at that time is like, 'Okay, we'll see. I'll take that challenge. Let's go.' You know, I became more aggressive, sometimes to the point where I would create failure because I was too aggressive. But do you understand what I mean by that? I mean, if somebody were to knock me down—and I'd get right back up. And then my desire to beat that guy was twice as much.

"Now, I played with a guy named George Hendrick, easiest-going guy in the world. The last thing you ever wanted to do was to wake that guy up by knocking him down, because here's a guy that went to Vietnam and got shot and killed a lot of people. He was a military guy. Okay, now all of a sudden you wake him up. I mean, the next couple of pitches, he'd come up to home plate, he's just hitting balls as hard as I've ever seen anybody hit them. And he was such an easygoing kind of guy and he was a good player. But boy, when you woke him up like that, he became aggressive. And no intimidations, like, 'Nobody's going to intimidate me, pal. I'll show you who's going to get intimidated!'

"I remember Frank Robinson, who was my hitting coach for the Orioles. And I always remember, he goes, 'Man, you never give in to that pitcher. He's going to knock you down—you've either got two choices: get up and hit him, or go out and beat the shit out of him.'

"That's what he used to say. 'You've got two choices. What are you going to do? Because that one falling backwards isn't going to work.' That's kind of the mental aggressiveness that I'm saying, that anger aggression that helped me at times really get through tight situations."

COMMENTARY—OVERCOMING FEAR

Doug's perspective is a strong "alpha male" point of view. It certainly worked for him. I suspect some women might find this mental approach somewhat disconcerting. It is not the only view presented here, but certainly speaks to what a lot of men feel, especially in more hostile, competitive, and combative situations.

The ability to overcome fear can be a major issue in anyone's life: fear of failure at work, in relationships, in business ventures, or on the field. Athletics touches us all, because we see players and teams in all sports battling to succeed. It is easy to become intimated by players and teams that appear to be better, stronger, or more talented. It is easy to become intimated by someone who seems stronger, more aggressive, and more intimidating. International politics are filled with threats and confrontations, with politicians hoping to create fear and force people or nations to back down. The drama of life is always filled with challenges to stand up for what you believe.

It has been said there that is no real courage without fear. Fear is a natural response when we feel threatened. It is how we deal with the fear that makes the difference, not whether or not we feel the fear. Fear can only be overcome by facing it head-on. How can you find this inner strength?

In addition, the emotion of fear is related to our primitive brain which is programmed for survival. The "fight or flight" response dumps a lot of adrenaline into our system when we feel threatened. Advanced meditation techniques like Kriya Yoga move the life force energy from the primitive brain, Medulla Oblongata, to higher centers in the brain. When you know how to consciously do this, you can mitigate your program instincts and maintain peace of mind.

Fear begins in the mind when we believe that something bad will happen to us: get physically hurt, die, get embarrassed, become shamed, be financially devastated, become homeless, or emotionally hurt. Our sense of self is often tied up with our achievements, and we think we will be worthless or "less than" if we do not win. Our sense of self is often connected to how others view us, so we are afraid to say what we really think or feel because we fear others will attack us for our beliefs. The truth is that we cannot control how others will react to what we do or say. Others may not like what we do, and sometimes others have more talent and ability than we do. However, it is our attachment to the outcome that basically creates fear in our mind. If we believe we will be fine, no matter what the outcome, then we can be free to overcome any initial fear that might arise in the mind.

Sometimes that fear can be so great that we feel paralyzed and unable to act. Fear releases chemicals in the body that have a strong effect. Sometimes we need a strong reaction to get our energy moving and take action. The initial bust of energy that comes from anger can be used constructively if positively directed. Wild lashing out is counter-productive—it usually just creates more problems; it does not solve problems. However, the focusing of anger to activate us into action can be a useful thing. It certainly helped Doug DeCinces.

However, ultimately it is a choice of how and what we do. We can be heroes or victims. If we choose to let our fear overwhelm us, then we become victims and let others take advantage of us. If we choose to stand up for what we believe and believe in ourselves, then we can be victorious. Once again, it is important to remember that a spiritual practice that establishes a strong and solid connection to the Self or soul, creates the necessary inner resources to withstand life's greatest challenges.

A strong self has a balance between the masculine and feminine. Some individuals have difficulty with strong masculine qualities, but these are important during times of conflict. We need to have an inner strength that allows us to stand up, speak up, and take action—not in a mean, vicious, and hurtful manner, but with strength of conviction and determination. Anger that is contained and focused becomes a powerful force. If you are afraid of your anger and have not mastered it, you will not be a powerful resource that will help you confront and master life's greatest challenges.

On a spiritual note, it has been said, "God helps those who help themselves." This means we have to act and cannot sit back and hope someone else—God, parents, or some authority—will solve our problems. We can experience divine intervention when we are doing our part, which requires a 110 percent commitment by us. When we act, unseen forces can be there to help us, to lead us, to speak through our intuition, and to empower us to succeed. Inspired performance is just that: "to affect, guide, or arouse by divine influence." When we know that divine influence is available, we do not feel alone in facing our most difficult challenges. Zack Johnson, the 2007 Master's Champion, won on Easter Sunday. He reported that he felt the presence of Jesus walking with him step-by-step on every hole. Was this his imagination—or not? Those who have experienced this type of divine help think not! As a final thought, Jesus was there to help and inspire; Jesus did not hit the golf ball! Zach's success was the result of individual talent and hard work as well as faith. We can accomplish great things when we have faith. The body cannot accomplish what the mind believes to be impossible. Zach Johnson came down the stretch and beat one of the best golfers in the world, Tiger Woods. The fear of intimidation could have been enough to wipe him off the course.

In essence, then, fear starts in the mind, and the challenge is to find a way to stay positive and believe you are capable of success. The depth of your heart and spiritual realization can also be a great source of support to overcome adversity. Your relationship with Spirit often gives you the extra faith, added resources, and inner strength to persevere and do your very best.

JIM BROWN

Jim Brown offers a slightly different perspective on fear:

"Fear of failure is probably the strongest fear that an athlete can have, and it's not always based upon your opponents. It's kind of based upon the expectation that people have of you. People create a level for you that you'll reach maybe one or two times, but they want you to reach it every time. So you know that you kind of peak when you reach that level one or two times, but now you go out there, and if you don't reach your level which they have established, then you sometimes consider failure. So that fear of failure is a big part of it."

COMMENTARY

Mr. Brown discusses a very important subject with regards to expectations. Expectations may be one of the greatest single factors that can lead to our undoing—although it can be a mixed blessing. On the one hand, if you hold a high expectation of someone's capabilities, then you can help them achieve great things. For example, there was a classic study done in the public school system a number of years ago on expectations and learning. Two identically matched groups of children were placed in two separate classrooms. Each teacher was given a different orientation regarding her students. One teacher was told that she was given a select group of the brightest students in the school. The other teacher was informed that she was given a select group of the worst performing students. Remember, the level of intelligence and past performance was actually the same between the groups. At the end of the year, the group that was labeled as high achievers actually performed better in the final test scores. The only difference was the expectation of the teacher.

If you want to see this reality in action, next time you are playing golf, just say to someone in your foursome, "I really expect you to make this one!"

Most people will be negatively affected by your statement and feel the pressure of your expectation. Most likely, they will not do their best. There is a big difference between saying, "I expect you to make it" and "I know you can make it." The latter is supportive and helpful, the former creates a burden and fear of failure.

Thus, if you are a coach or parent, it is helpful to hold a vision of the highest potential for your players or child. There are a variety of theories that attempt to explain this reality. One theory comes from the world of quantum physics. At the quantum level, everything is energy—matter and consciousness. Several very interesting studies were performed in which electrons were observed and found to show up at different locations, or not at all, depending upon the observer. The "uncertainty principle," as it is called, suggests that human consciousness interacts to determine what we perceive. Thus, when you hold an expectation of someone, your thoughts and awareness—which are consciousness—help to determine the reality that manifests. Although these forces are unseen to the naked eye, it does not mean they do not exist. Remember, you cannot see radio and TV waves, either.

Given what we know about energy and consciousness, it is less mysterious how this strange process unfolds. Because thought is energy—and we are all, at the most essential level, energy—we pick up or absorb these energy fields and become influenced by them. If an individual is very aware and sensitive to subtle impressions, he or she can actually feel this happening.

Expectations can lead to your undoing. Expectations, when combined with attachment, can result in great suffering. If you have some preconceived idea regarding how you are supposed to perform, and you don't live up to your expectations, you may have a host of reactions: disappointment, frustration, anger, despair, embarrassment, humiliation, or a lowering of self-esteem. There is also usually some anticipatory anxiety or fear about not being able to live up to these expectations. As Jim Brown tells us, if you become emotionally invested in what others think about you, embrace those ideas, and then create some idea about how you are supposed to perform, you are in trouble! Remember—it is the attachment to the outcome that creates the big problem. If you have an idea of how you want to perform, are not overly attached to the outcome, and can maintain your focus in the present moment, then you will have a clearer mind and a much better chance to succeed.

Peak performance is enabled when you are not thinking about the future and are able to keep your focus in the moment—in the here and now. Being in the present opens a gateway for a mind/body connection that transcends the rational mind. You need to be free and open to be at your best. Fear creates contraction and hesitation. By definition, it presupposes that you are experiencing a state of separation from your deeper Self and the Divine. Fear does not exist in a unified state of consciousness!

Times of crisis often result in profound life changes. You go through a process and come out the other side changed and transformed by your experience. You may become wiser, more compassionate, more humble, more self-confident, or more loving. Whatever the change, you probably could not predict it at the beginning. All you felt was your life falling apart: your ideas about yourself, what you do, or who you think you should be. Only by fully trusting in life's process and living in the moment can you be fully present to live each moment, each day, and see where you are taken. You have to let go to get to where you are going. This process of letting go also requires letting go of preconceived ideas and expectations about how things should turn out. Letting go is not easy. It takes a depth of inner wisdom, trust, and realization. It is easier to develop these qualities when life is good, rather than in the midst of personal breakdown. However, oftentimes it takes a personal crisis to open the inner doors to these realizations.

On Doubt

Doubt is another factor that undermines our ability to maintain a positive mental outlook. Lee Brandon has some helpful things to share on how she manages doubt. I asked, "Do you ever have doubt? Does that ever come up in your life in terms of your ability to be successful?"

Interview
Lee Brandon on Doubt

"No. Failure's not an option. Failure's never been an option. And if something feels like a failure, I like using the adage, 'Well, if I can't do it, then I'll bulldoze through it, I'll dig a hole under it, I'll climb over it.' To me, I'll find a way to explore every option, because quitting is not an option. And if, at that point in time, the answer is still 'no,' then I'll reevaluate. But to me, sometimes the universe's answer is 'no,' but maybe it's just, 'no, not now.' Because to me, every successful person I've ever seen has never taken 'no'—ever. They never quit the first time they run into an obstacle—never. None of them — none of the greats. If you read anything about history, it's all about people who found a way to persevere and be resourceful and go around everything that was thrown at them.

"If you continue moving yourself—the law of probability—your probabilities of being successful are greater if you continue to move. As soon as you sit still, nothing's going to hit you, and nothing will land in your lap. It's all about pursuing the next angle. You put a bunch of BBs in a pan and you shake them—they're all hitting each other. So I think a lot of people often become isolated.

"I call it the ingrown toenail complex. It's easy, and it's easy to get stuck in inertia or feel like it's hard to overcome that stuck place. But all it takes is one step, and then all of a sudden, you're back in the game again. You've just got to just keep moving. Reevaluate. Don't be unrealistic about the goals. Like, I'm always reevaluating my goals, but I'm always proactive. I'm always bulldozing over or under, and moving, and maybe that's a lot of extra energy that maybe is not real focused on my behalf, and I'd be the first one to admit that, that maybe not every angle I've pursued is the best angle. But I'm having fun, and there's something to be said for that."

DICK FOSBURY ON THE POWER OF THE MIND

During my interview with Dick Fosbury, we discussed the power of the mind to create both positive and negative states:

"Well, even now that you mention that—even the opposite I think is true. For example, where you can be very negative, and you can make yourself sick. Clearly, when I'm having a tough time, like this week, I'm very stressed out, I'm overloaded, and so every day, there are very negative thoughts to deal with. 'I don't want to be here, and I don't want to be doing this stuff'— and most times, within a couple days, I'll usually get sick. The problem is, of course, is that you don't necessarily control it, and you can make yourself really sick, and that's one of my fears is that, well, I would really like to have somebody besides myself take control and say, 'Okay, Dick, you need to take a break.' I'm not responsible for saying that, you know, I really can't do all of this stuff right now, I'd rather somebody else just do that, and making myself sick kind of takes it out my responsibility. And so I think you can go both ways very easily."

COMMENTARY

Dick is discussing a very important issue here. We have the power to affect our health. Kaiser Permanente did a classic study a number of years ago in their medical centers. People were screened prior to their visit to a physician, and the results were striking: 80 percent of all visits to a doctor were stress-related. What starts in the mind goes into your emotions and then into your body. If you can learn to resolve the tension and conflict that begins in your mind, you can create a much healthier life. Think about it. Most of our emotional reactions are the result of our inability to just accept what is happening. We make judgments about how life should be going. We make judgments about other people's behavior or other people's attitudes. We have preferences about the weather, about how much money we should have, how we look, etc. The list goes on and on. Physical health begins in the mind with a clear inner life and an acceptance of what is. Unfortunately, many people do not even strive to achieve this state of inner peace and acceptance. It appears that they are more interested in coercing the world and everybody around them to comply with their ideas of perfection than finding a way to live in harmony.

It is true that you have the power to create a better life by creating a positive inner reality. At the very least, if you do not react emotionally to the ups and downs of your life, you will have great peace of mind and physical well-being.

ON USING THE POWER OF THE MIND FOR MANIFESTATION

The popularity of The Secret appears to be the result of people hoping to create more abundance through the power of the mind. Your thoughts can create a positive field of energy that will impact your life. You can become a magnet to attract positive experiences. The nature of your consciousness determines your ability to actually manifest. The Secret does not provide an in-depth discussion about this. Just because you visualize something does not necessarily mean it will come into manifestation. The fact is that your powers for manifestation are related to the degree of your realization. The clearer you are (less in ego consciousness) and the more you are able to maintain concentrated focus, the more power you have to impact your reality. Spiritual practices which use meditation, pranayam (life force control) techniques, devotion, and prayer do increase your powers of concentration and alignment with Spirit—the deeper your attunement, the greater your ability to manifest.

Karma does come into play in these circumstances. Sometimes we do have forces acting upon us from previous circumstances, either in this lifetime or beyond. These circumstances have to be played out, and these forces can make life difficult at times. We have to deal with the issues at hand and move on. Just because you visualize something does not guarantee that you will get it. Quite honestly, this is a rather childish understanding. Your degree of realization does make a difference. However, maintaining a positive state of mind and holding the vision of what you want does help during difficult times. It might just take longer than you would like and you might need to put more willpower into your effort. The most important thing to remember is: don't ever give up!

It is worthwhile to note that grace transcends karma. So your prayers and positive thinking can draw God's response to help you during difficult times. Do not be discouraged or think something is wrong with you if you don't get exactly what you are trying to manifest. Life is more complicated. Keep deepening your connection with Spirit and doing everything in your power to be the best you can be. Keep your faith and eventually you will come out the other side. Remember, if you don't like your life circumstance, then work on changing it from the inside out!

You may be familiar with applied kinesiology. It's a muscle testing process to see how the body reacts to various influences. I wanted to show the girls on the UCLA golf team how any one individual player is actually affected by the group consciousness. I had one of the girls stand up in front of the group, I said, "Okay, I want you to think of yourself as a great player." We did the muscle testing and she was real strong. Then I said, "All right, now think you're a terrible player." Her arm collapsed. She just had no capacity to keep her arm up. So then I said to everybody in the room, "I want you to look at Susan here, and I want you to hold her in your mind as the greatest contributor to your team and think that you're so happy she's here." And then I had Susan do the muscle test, and her arm was strong. And then I said, "Okay, now I want you to think of Susan as the worst player—you wish she was not even on your team." And she would collapse. I said to the team, "You know, how you conceive of each other makes a difference in terms of how each person plays," because I knew they had some interpersonal problems going on. And I said, "So when you're out there and you start thinking about somebody, think positive. Send them some positive thoughts, because it will help them." And that was the first time they went to Nationals, and they came in fifth. And the coach said, "You know, the team was so connected and they were so focused. There was something going on there." This is a great story that speaks to the power of collective consciousness.

SELF-ANALYSIS—POSITIVE STATE OF MIND

Answer the following questions: True or False

1. I often doubt my abilities.

2. I do not mentally prepare before I must perform.

3. I am not confident in my abilities.

4. I often have negative thoughts about the future.

5. I become negative in the face of adversity.

6. I am easily overcome by fear.

7. I do not believe that my mental outlook affects my body.

8. I do not believe that I can invoke the presence of Spirit for help and protection.

9. I do not have a strong mind that can stay focused.

10. I doubt that I can overcome defeat and adversity.

11. I am very afraid to fail.

12. I am easily influenced by other people's expectations.

13. I do not believe my mental outlook can influence the quality of my life.

14. I do not expect good things to come my way.

If you answered "true" to two or more of the above items, you may need to do some personal work in the area of positive mental states.

Directions for Corrections

If you have identified the lack of a positive mental state as a potential roadblock to your capacity for high functioning, then create the following action plan:

1. Obtain a life coach to help you speed up your process for change.

2. Begin a daily mindful awareness/introspection practice, and just watch what your mind generates.

3. Clarify your mental "tapes" that hold negative beliefs and expectations.

4. Develop a few positive affirmations and repeat them many times a day:

   a. The power of Spirit is within me. I can accomplish whatever I need.

   b. I am strong and will overcome all of life's challenges.

   c. I will receive everything I need to accomplish my goals.

5. Keep a written diary of your daily progress.

6. Begin each day by asking your higher power to help you become more positive.

7. Use self-hypnosis to reprogram you subconscious mind.

CHAPTER 4

THE FOURTH PRINCIPLE:

YOUR ABILITY TO ADJUST ALLOWS YOU TO ADAPT TO NEW AND CHANGING REALITIES

Let's review what has already been stated about adjustment. Change is a natural part of life. Your ability to adjust and adapt to new situations is vital to the ability to respond to change. The most adaptive response requires that you live in the moment and effectively interact with what is. If you get caught in responding to what you wish reality to be, rather than to what reality is, then you might find yourself left behind. Buck Rodgers speaks to this issue very directly, and you will hear more about that later. However, for now it is important to realize that success over time requires the ability to adapt to changing circumstances. Mental and emotional rigidity impairs you from adjusting to new and different situations. If you become overwhelmed with fear, you will be frozen like a deer in the headlights. Your ability to adjust can determine how quickly you adapt to new circumstances. When the world is changing around you and you don't change, you can be in serious trouble.

If you have any doubt that the world is changing, just turn on the TV and watch the news or read a newspaper. President Trump just created a potential trade war with Mexico. He issued a visa ban for individuals from a select number of Middle Eastern Counties. Harvard University just issued a travel warning for students and faculty against international travel. Major claims of voting fraud are made without any actually factual support. Conspiracy theories run wild and "alternative facts" are now offered as reality. Is Russia going to be our best friend? Where is all this going? We don't know! One thing is for sure, "The times, they are a changing." If there was ever a time to learn how to adjust, welcome to the present!

Adjustment requires movement. You have to make a change and do something differently—hence, movement. If you are frozen in fear, you will not be able to act. Fear can be a good thing, because it is a warning that danger is approaching, and you need to wake up and act. If you wait too long, fear can consume and overwhelm you so you cannot move. Your body will be filled with so much adrenaline that your brain and muscles are in lockdown. If you recognize the warning function of fear and are able to effectively respond, then you are in good shape. Many of the following principles will relate to overcoming fear, but for now it is imperative to realize that success often requires change and adjusting to new circumstances.

Interview
Buck Rodgers

Buck Rodgers had a lot to say about the ability to adjust. We were talking about what is takes to be a successful ball player. He said, "The people who have great ability that don't make it are usually the ones who do not have the ability to adjust. You have to adjust at every level. If it's not working this way, you got to say, 'well, let's try it this way.' And pretty soon you find something that works. And if you're not afraid of change, you got some ability—you don't have to have the greatest ability, I certainly didn't—you got a chance to stick around."

It is important to realize that you have to be flexible and open to change. Notice that Buck said, "If you are not afraid of change." Some people are. They are worried that things will get worse, so they want everything to stay the same, or they are worried that they will not be able to be successful in a different circumstance. Of course, there is always just plain laziness, because it does take additional physical, emotional, and mental energy to adjust to new circumstances.

I asked Buck, "How do you think you learn about that ability to change? Some people are kind of rigid."

Buck shared his thoughts on this, saying, "Well, I think it was all my bringing-up—family. I was in a small town; I did a lot of farm work. When something breaks down, you go get some bailing wire; you tie it up, and you adjust. You got to make it work for the day. You can't say, 'all right, all the work's done today, because the tie on the wagon came off.' It might rain that night and wash out the whole crop. You got to find some way to get it done. I'm thankful every day that I was brought up in a small town, because we had to make those decisions even as kids.

"I don't like excuse-makers. Golfers are the worst guys in the world for making excuses. God almighty! 'The bird tweeted, the surface, the greens aren't the same, the wind's blowing, the fairways are in bad shape, I got a bad lie in the rough.' Golfers are the worst I've ever seen—before they ever hit the ball. That's why I love Tiger Woods. I've never heard Tiger Woods make an excuse. I mean, he goes out there and won't make an excuse for the greens being too fast. But you got these other crybabies, like John Daly and everyone else—he's defeated before he starts. He's got an excuse for being bad. Before he ever starts, he's already defeated, because he's already got his reason why [he] lost the thing. They're amazing.

"But I found out real soon that a lot of guys didn't make it because they were satisfied with being mediocre. And they couldn't make that adjustment to go that next jump. And they were satisfied with being the two-league hitter or two-sixty hitter. A lot of these guys had the God-given ability, but psychologically, they couldn't handle it, because they couldn't make that adjustment. The ability to adjust is very important."

As our interview continued, Buck began talking about the mental toughness of today's baseball players as compared to the Japanese. "I just don't think the modern generation in general has the mental toughness of a lot of years ago. And whether it's been too easy, whether it's because one thing or another, I got my opinions, but I don't know if I'm right or it's one thing or another. So it's like different areas of the country, which are more mentally tough than others."

"Where do you see that?" I asked. "Which part of the country?"

He responded, "I think this, the Northwest, I think we're a little bit—I think this is probably the worst. Southern California, I think is probably the least mentally tough, the most spoiled. And I include me and my kids in that bunch."

"Do you think it's because the weather's easier, the life is easier?"

"I think it's everything. I just think you've got everything at your touch— you want the beaches, you want the mountains, you want the desert, you've got everything right there. Now if you're in the South, or any other part of the country, you've got to make a concentrated effort to go places, do things. It's not around the corner. I think just about everything you want—it's just right around the corner."

"It is easier out here," I said.

"Sure," he answered. "And I don't think the ability to make the adjustment—you don't have to make the adjustment, very little. I mean, just going from summer, to fall, to winter, where you have to take the storm windows out and put them up or put them in the thing or bring one down, the other up—I mean, whatever way you got to do it, those are adjustments. Maybe minor—chopping wood or bringing the wood in for the wood-burning fireplace. Whatever you have to do to adjust from summer, to fall, to winter, back to spring — those are adjustments that most of the people here never do. We get our windows washed after the rains, and then hopefully sometime in the summer again. But now the rains have started—prematurely started, I mean—there's no adjustment. Check your roof, whatever. But they're all minor. Not because we're a bunch of wusses, but because our lifestyle dictates that we don't have to make too many adjustments. Now financially, yeah, you might have to make some financial adjustments. You lose your job, that's the same all over. Your house burns down, that's the same all over. But I don't think that on a day-to-day basis, you have to make that many adjustments. And I think if you're from Southern California, if you've been here for any length of time, you'll have a tough time going someplace where they have to make adjustments. I mean, how many people out here, ordinary people, have a spring, summer, fall, and winter wardrobe? Most of them wear the same clothes year-round. Back there, you got to bring out the coats and the boots and the galoshes and the umbrellas."

"That's an interesting point. I used to direct a program for international citizen diplomacy during the eighties, and I took Americans into the Soviet Union on peace missions. Americans had a lot of trouble adjusting to a different culture."

"Sure, we spent three weeks in Italy, and we spent almost three weeks in Japan, and of course, I've been to the Dominican, I managed there—and Venezuela, I managed there, and I managed in Canada for eight years. When you go to Italy, somebody is boisterous, and they just can't make the adjustment. They say, 'Hey! I've never had this hard bread. The bread is too hard. We don't have it where I'm from.' You sit there and think, wow. Not that tough. But they can't make the adjustment."

COMMENTARY

This idea of adjustment seems simple, but it is really a profound concept regarding life success. Of course, we have all heard the layperson's definition of insanity: "Keep doing the same thing and expect different results!"

Our inability to adjust to new and changing circumstances begins in our mind. We believe that we have the right way to do something and are determined to stay with our convictions. The wise individual will adjust his or her thinking when given new information. Other times, we are attached to our comfort zone. We are afraid to change and try new things because we are out of our comfort zone. We don't know what the outcome will be and are afraid to try something new and find out. So we continue to do the same thing, hoping for a different result.

We become stuck in old and familiar patterns that are comfortable, even though they may be non-productive. For example, we get used to the speed of the greens, and the conditions change—rain has softened and slowed the speed. We cannot seem to hit the putt a little firmer, because we are mentally stuck in an image and memory of how hard to swing.

Change requires some mental work to reorganize our thinking and perceptions. We have to become accustomed to a new way of doing something or a new way of feeling. We have to be wiling to take a chance and trust the new approach. In essence, we have to be willing to make a mistake to find out if the new approach will work. Change sometimes requires us to develop a new sense of self. We might have to restructure our lives or our business. It is easier to just keep the same old behaviors, beliefs, and thought patterns.

Years ago when I was a member at Mt. Gate Country Club, I met a new member who was a professional actor and former Minor League professional baseball player. He was part of the New York Yankee farm system. He confided in me that he was never called up to the majors in spite of the fact that he was a very successful pitcher. I asked him if he had any idea why they did not call him up, given his success and talent. He said they told him that he drank too much and was too wild with women. He said, "I could not stay in my room and read the Bible, I had too much energy to release!" This is an unfortunate but good example of someone who could have had a career in Major League professional baseball if he had the desire and ability to adjust.

LEARN TO LIVE IN THE PRESENT

The ability to adjust is tantamount to living in the present. Adjustments in life require you to make quick assessments and quick changes. You have to be awake, alert, mentally sharp, and fully present to make quick changes. If you are mentally asleep, afraid to lose, afraid to make mistakes, or are insecure, then it will take you forever to adjust. You may be able to change, but by the time you are ready, it may be too late.

If you are a boxer, you don't have a lot of time to think about changing. Your survival may count on a quick adjustment to a different approach from your opponent. If you are up at bat at the bottom of the ninth with men on base and a new pitcher comes in, you don't have a lot of time to adjust.

The ability to live in the moment is perhaps one of the most important skills you can develop. Living in the moment opens a doorway into an expanded universe. When each moment is fresh and you are able to respond to the reality at hand, then your choices are multiplied. When you have a fixed response style with a mentally rigid approach, you then become predictable, boring, and outdated. Life is constantly evolving, and if you cannot adjust to these changes, then you will be left behind. Think about it—what if you are a pitcher and always throw the same pitch when you are in trouble? How long do you think the opposition will take to figure that out?

Individuals have written complete books just on this topic of how to live in the moment. Learning to live in the present is a spiritual discipline all by itself. Living in the present demands that you get out of your ego—the mentality that is fixed on what it believes to be true. If you are stuck in how something should be, you are not free to experience what something is. Raising children is a very difficult task, especially during adolescence (theirs, not yours—although if you are an adolescent raising an adolescent, then you have double trouble!). Every generation is evolving and changing. If you hold the mentality that your kids should behave like you did when you were young, it will be impossible for you to relate to them! You will be relating to who you think they should be.

If you believe any of the literature on the evolution of consciousness and spiritual awareness, then living in the moment becomes even more important. The ego is what limits us and traps us into only perceiving the obvious physical and material realities—the more subtle realms of higher wisdom, intuitive knowing, and subtle energy are unavailable. Consciousness is not rigid. It is very fluid, spacious, and open. It has a foundation in trust, surrender, faith, and love. The ego is controlling, rigid, and limited. It has its foundation in fear.

Look at any great golf professional. He or she is trying to win a tournament and coming down the backstretch. There is a par five with a dogleg left over water to the green. A big hitter can make it in two with a great shot over the water. The risk is great—a bogey or more—and the reward is an eagle. The eagle may determine the win. It takes a full and fluid swing to make those shots; fear will unravel even the greatest player. However, wisdom can be an even greater ally than fearlessness. Wisdom based on self-knowledge is powerful. Zach Johnson, 2007 Master's Champion, laid up on every par five. He made lots of birdies on those holes. He knew his limits, capitalized on his strengths, and came out on top.

The ability to adjust is huge. If you are playing on the tour every day and one week you are on fast greens that have dried out because of winds and the next week you are playing on slower greens with a lot of moisture, you have to adjust. If you don't, then all your putts will be short.

If you are in the business world and have a great company that prints books on a traditional printing press, what do you do when someone invents digital printing and the world no longer relies on traditional printing methods? Do you adjust or go out of business?

If you are at bat in the bottom of the ninth with two men on base and your team is one run behind, what do you do when the relief pitcher comes in for the close? Do you adjust to a new pitcher or just act like the previous pitcher is throwing strikes at you?

Let me share one last story on this subject. A number of years ago I invested in an Arizona company that did condo conversion in Houston,

Texas. The company went out of business and took $8 million of the $10 million I and seventy-two other investors put into the project. This company left us with a partially rehabilitated 136-unit complex that needed another $3.3 million to complete. The market value of the property was then estimated to be less than $2 million. That was the hard reality. We all lost a lot of money. I accepted the new reality and spent a lot of time finding a buyer to bail us out at $2.7 million. Now remember, we have seventy-two investors in this project who do not know each other. We were passive investors and now were forced to be partners in a homeowners' association. Since each person owned his or her units, we needed a 100 percent agreement to sell the entire property. Some of the investors in this group were elderly and lost a lot of money. Others were not that old but did not want to accept the reality that this project was not worth what they invested. I found a buyer for $2.7 million, and a handful of people refused to adjust to the new reality and said no to the deal. A few months later, the group was out of cash to pay insurance and security, which is required by the city. The offer went to down to $1.7 million, and some still refuse to sell. The future appeared to be rather bleak with the prospect that the city would condemn this undeveloped property, which had become an eyesore in a nice neighborhood. It seemed highly possible that we would get nothing for this property and lose everything. This is a great example of people unable to accept new circumstances and adjust to the current reality. These few individuals created ideas about value that were not supported by real facts and were attached to old realities, and they refused to accept their losses and move on. This failure to adjust could have cost us all a lot of money. A few years later reality sank in and the group finally agreed to sell for the original price offered. People did adjust, but it took them a long time to do so.

In summary, the ability to adjust requires mental alertness, flexibility, adaptability, and non-attachment. If you learn to adjust, you may find it a lot easier to accept and deal with change.

In the first book, *Bouncing Back*, the economy was the biggest issue. Now we have a new political situation and the economy. Jobs and national security are important but there is also a new element, ethics and morality. Whatever your views, it is easy to get stuck and discount new information. We seem to be living in a world that values one's beliefs more than the facts. In order for us to find some common ground and make good decisions for all Americans, we need to accept and adjust to our new reality, whether you like it or not. We can all benefit if we can let go of rigid preconceived ideas and perceptions and take a fresh look at reality. Not distorted made up reality, but observable, verifiable reality that will allow for a mature discussion leading to good decisions. We are not back in Kansas anymore and the wizard my not have all the answers.

SELF-ANALYSIS—ADJUSTMENT

Answer the following questions: True or False

1. When I think of trying something new or different, I often feel afraid.

2. I am afraid to make mistakes.

3. I tend to repeat familiar patterns and behaviors, even if they do not seem to work out well.

4. I have a tendency to try to hold on to what I have achieved.

5. I do not like to change.

6. I can be a little lazy.

7. I resist other people's ideas.

8. I believe my ideas are the best.

9. I find it difficult to find solutions for new problems.

10. I get angry when things do not go as I expected.

11. I find myself getting stuck in old and familiar patterns of thinking and behavior.

12. I typically do what is most comfortable.

13. I often mistrust my own gut feelings.

14. I am very cautious about trying new things.

15. I am not very interested in feedback from others.

If you answered, "true" to two or more of the above items, you may need to do some personal work in the area of adjustment.

DIRECTIONS FOR CORRECTIONS

If you have identified adjustment as a potential roadblock to your capacity for high functioning, then create the following action plan:

1. Obtain a life coach to help you speed up your process for change.

2. Begin a daily introspection process in which you identify any psychological blocks to being more flexible and adventurous:

   a. Fear of failure.

   b. Fear of loss and abandonment.

   c. Any tendency to be lazy.

   d. Any underlying depression that robs your life force and your energy.

   e. Rigid thinking patterns in which you think life should be a certain way.

   f. An unwillingness to admit mistakes and initiate self-action for correction.

3. Prioritize the above issues and begin to systematically address them one at a time.

4. Keep a written diary of your daily progress.

5. Try something new every day.

6. Develop a daily meditative/contemplative practice that assesses your willingness to change.

7. Make a conscious decision to listen to your intuition and follow it! Begin small!

8. Begin each day by asking your higher power to guide and direct your life according to the divine plan.

Chapter 5

The Fifth Principle:

Your Capacity to Rise Above Your Conditioning and Societal Pressures Will Unleash Your Personal Power

Carl Jung coined the term "individuation" to describe the higher end of psychological maturity. He suggested that more mature individuals have progressed beyond their early childhood conditioning. Moreover, they are also able to separate from and transcend societal ideas, values, and pressures when those things are limiting, unhealthy, or non-productive.

An important part of growing up is to learn to think independently of others, especially authority figures. The voice of wisdom is often different from the norm. New ideas and solutions are not typically generated from business as usual. Independent thinking and an ability to be emotionally secure allow for new possibilities. When you merely act as you were taught and believe what everyone else is saying, you may be limiting your growth and potential for more adaptive action. The wisest and more adaptive individuals have the inner strength and mental clarity to perceive what is right for them in that moment. They are not merely following old conditioning and blending in with convention.

An important process in personal development is to be able to think independently based on your own wisdom and core values. Oftentimes this may set you apart from others. It will certainly test your sense of self and strength of character.

Doug DeCinces' story continues here, and he speaks directly to this issue. We were discussing overcoming life's difficulties when he shared the following:

Interview
Doug DeCinces

"I had difficulties playing the game. You know, I had confrontations with Earl Weaver [the Orioles' manager]. I ended up going to a psychologist when I was going through all these different things, and it was probably way before anybody's time of knowing that a professional athlete would go see a psychologist to work through some things. And one of the things was that Earl was just a dominating force in that dugout, mentally; he had your career, and he would say things and be … and not all of them are positive, trust me. You know, he'd shake your hand every time you hit a three-run home run or you made a nice defensive play, because that's what he expected you to do.

"But it's all those other times. Let me tell you, it wasn't easy. And there were a lot of rookies that would come through who folded—couldn't play for the guy and would either go back to the minors or they'd trade them, because Earl figured out—his theory was that, 'If you can't play, if I'm upsetting you, then I don't want you up with bases loaded in the bottom of the ninth inning; because, you know, you've got to be able to handle me and play the game the way I want you to play the game, or I don't want you on my team.' And that was kind of his theory.

"I was raised—you do not disrespect your elders. I just kept taking this abuse—this verbal abuse—and taking it too personal, is really what I was doing; taking a lot, and then trying to replace Brooks Robinson, and having the negativity on top of that, and everything. I can remember talking just recently with Brooks Robinson a couple of years ago, and we were playing golf together. And he said, 'You know, a lot of us veterans'—because I was the only rookie on the team, too; they were all All-Star veteran guys—so he said, 'You know, we could never understand why Earl was always riding you so hard.' He goes, 'One time I went up to him and told him, "Back off of him." '

"And I said, 'You said that?'

"And he goes, 'Yeah. I told him to back off of you, because it was abnormal how much he was doing what he was doing.'

"I think Earl had a problem—that he looked at me as this guy that was taking his favorite player's position, because you know what? Brooks Robinson helped make Earl Weaver who he was. And Earl had a hard time letting go. And as history proved out, he kept giving Brooks every single opportunity. You know, I'd play second base and shortstop and then back to third. I'd play first and then back to third. I'd go all over the place. But I was just happy to get the opportunity to play back then as a rookie. But on the same token, I never got the, 'Hey, kid, I'm behind you. Let's go do it.' Earl's theory was, 'I put your name in the lineup. Get your ass out there and play. And you'd better be playing the way I want you to play.'

"So what happened is I finally stood up to the guy. When he unduly attacked me, I just said, 'That's enough.' And I wouldn't have probably been able to do that if I hadn't gone through some work to recognize that I had to be able to stand on my own feet and not allow somebody to berate me and do those things. It was almost like kind of an abusive situation.

"I really lost it—almost punched him right there in the dugout. If it wasn't for a policeman and a couple of players, I was going after him, you know? And he recognized then that he had gone too far. And it was the first game of a double header. And it was the year after Brooks Robinson retired. And I came to spring training, and my wife had miscarried the first day of spring training. I missed five days. I came out, and the very first ground ball I took at third base took a bad hop and broke my nose. I had to have surgery. I missed the first three weeks of spring training.

"Then I come out, and Earl says, 'You know what? We have this young kid, Eddie Murray. I want to get him into the lineup. I want you to go play second base.' Now, I went through three-plus years of replacing Brooks Robinson. First year he's not in uniform, you ask me to go play second base. Eddie screws up. He can't play defensively there. Obviously history proves he's one of the great baseball players in the game, and one of my dear teammates, one of the great offensive players the game has ever seen. But third base he was not. And after making a bunch of errors on the first trip and we lose all three games in Milwaukee, next thing you know I'm back at third.

"Now, Earl's trying to get—he's always bouncing things around, trying to get more power into the lineup, so then I go back to second. Then I go back to third. I go back to second, back to third. Finally I was to play at second base, and he's screaming and yelling. And I came off the field and I asked Lee May, I said, 'Who's he mad at?' And he points at me.

"And I go, 'What did I do?' and he goes, raises his hands like, I don't know. And he came up yelling, and I finally lost it—said, 'You talking to me?'

"And he goes, 'Damned right,' and he hit me with his finger in my chest. So I grabbed a hold of his hand. I wouldn't let go.

"I said, 'You ever touch me again—it will be the last thing you do.'

"I started to lose it. And he just tried to keep grabbing his hand, and I wouldn't let go of it. And I finally let go and he said, 'Smith, you're playing second base.'

"And I said, 'And Smith's playing second base the rest of the year.' I said, 'I'm no longer playing second base for you.'

"So anyway, argument over; he recognized I got the better of him in front of the team, and so he's not done with me. He comes after me in the hallway, and I—if it wasn't for a policeman, I probably would have been suspended from baseball for a while.

"But the funny thing is—is what's interesting about that story is the mental approach that happened during that time. I mean, I then said, 'I'm not taking anymore. I'd taken it from the fans. I'd taken it from Brooks. And I'm here to compete, and I'm not going to let somebody get in my way of becoming who I needed, who I want to become.'

"And so he has his meeting in between the double header and says, 'Well, sometimes I recognize … I expect all of you guys to be competitive, and sometimes I may push and say the wrong things. But I'm here to tell you I don't hold a grudge. I want to win just as bad as you want to win.'

"And so the lineup is posted, and I'm playing third base, second game. Palmer's going for his two hundredth victory. In the seventh inning, 0–0, I doubled off the right center field wall to knock in two runs. And I'm out there, and all of a sudden Rich Dauer, who had just been called up, he comes out to second base to pinch run for me. And he can't outrun me. And I said, 'What are you doing here?'

"And he goes—he's afraid. He's afraid I'm going to go off on him, you know? And he just says, 'Hey, the little guy sent me out.' He goes, 'Don't take it out on me.'

So I started coming out. I walked off the field. And I had all those emotions building up again. And I'll remember, 'I don't hold any grudges'—story. And Lee May jumped out of the dugout—he was the DH that game—grabbed a hold of me and he goes, 'Remember, the little guy doesn't hold any grudges. And you're going with me, and don't you say a word to anybody.'

"You know, Lee's a big man. He made me laugh. And that was kind of the way it was. From then on that year, I ended up having twenty-eight home runs and became my own baseball player. The second half of the season was one of the best seasons of my career. And it took that mental breakthrough."

I asked, "What do you think allowed you to make that shift?"

"Recognizing that even though I was raised to always respect your elders—you know what? That's a great trait, but I was an elder in my own right, and there comes a time where you stand up and you don't allow anybody to mistreat you. And I think I was allowing things to happen, and I was not comfortable. You know, just finally all that came out. Maybe it was the pressure of all the fans all the time, replacing Brooks Robinson—all those things were weighing on me.

"And I wasn't playing well. I'll be the first to admit. It was like, 'Okay, where am I playing today?' Sometimes I'd switch twice in a game. I'd start at second, go to third, finish at second, or go to third, second, and maybe then go to short. Offensively I was doing okay—but no, I really wasn't; I was kind of inconsistent. I think Earl thinks because I had that great second half, his whole theory was to piss me off and I'll play better, because later in the times when if I wasn't playing, he would come and attack me, trying to get me pissed off. And one of the coaches came up and said, 'Doug, he's just trying to get you pissed off. Don't worry about it.' You know, that was his 'It happened once, so maybe I can do it again'-type deal. But it didn't. I think at that point in time, I had grown through that.

"But it was, as I look back, a real turning point—a real turning point. I think those were two turning points in my career that allowed me to go on and become a successful major league baseball player. I mean, as you well know, just playing in the big leagues, the odds of playing there and staying are so enormous. But then to have all that other stuff put on top of you, you know—it's tough enough facing the pitchers, not have to face 36,000 fans and the pitcher when you're at home, and a manager."

COMMENTARY

The noted psychologist Carl Jung wrote volumes on personality theory and psychological development. I have always found his concept of individuation especially useful. Doug DeCinces' initiation into adulthood, and a resulting successful career in professional baseball, can be more fully understood from this point of view.

Dr. Jung suggests that part of growing up and maturing into adulthood requires a break from the prevalent surrounding authority figures. This break may be from parents and/or society's values.

I remember when I was a teenager seeking advice from my father, who was a physician trained in internal medicine. His medical training forced him to develop a style in which he always sounded like an expert, even if he was not very knowledgeable about the topic at hand. On this particular occasion, I was asking him for some advice about something that was very important to me at that time. I remember the moment when I realized he had no idea as to what he was talking about. I remember saying, "I really need some advice, but I don't need lousy advice. This is my life we are talking about!" In that moment, my relationship with my father shifted, and I no longer unconditionally deferred to him as the "expert."

Jung suggests that in order to fully grow and mature into adulthood, we must break with the surrounding convention or wisdom and embrace our individual feelings and beliefs. The recognition of our own truth gives us power to think, feel, and act as an individual and contribute from our unique sense of expression. Original thought, creative ideas, and even playing baseball are done at the highest level when the actions spring from an inner depth of authenticity. Our real power resides within an authentic self, and often it takes courage to stand up and fight for our right to exist. All too often, when we defer to outer authority as the true authority, we then find ourselves—individually and collectively as a society—being led down a wrong path. For example, our current economic, security, and political reality challenges our ability for independent thinking. We have a newly elected president that tells us, "Trust me, I will make America great again." He says whatever he wants, whenever he wants. He promises us the great wall and the moon. Do we just sit back and obediently obey and follow his dictates? Or do we become self-empowered with critical thinking, real analysis, and speak up for positions and solutions that are reasonable and have a good chance for success. Democracy requires its citizens to be well informed, engaged, and respectfully confront opposing ideas and positions. Be patriotic. Speak up and empower yourself.

Mr. DeCinces was, in a way, ahead of his time by consulting with a psychologist. He demonstrated his coach-ability—not only at a physical level, but also at a psychological one, as well. It was a wise choice, because it gave him the support and psychological understanding that his respect of elders was appropriate for him as a child, but not as an adult if it required him to abdicate his sense of self. It is impossible to do anything well if we do not have an authentic connection with our deeper self!

If you only take away one idea from this entire book, this one is worth keeping: You cannot excel if you do not honor and respect who you are! Honor and respect means that you express yourself; you honor your life and existence by being who you really are. Do not let other people undermine you, convince you that you cannot achieve your goals, that you do not know what you really feel, or that you do not know what is best for you. If you give up your self, if you give up your power, if you give up your inner knowing, you will pay a price, either emotionally or physically. Dick Fosbury is another good example of this truth. He was able to trust himself and allow his flop to organically evolve over time. During the Olympics, he did not allow the negative criticism and skepticism of the Russian and European coaches to derail him. His intuitive sense continued to guide and direct him and keep him on the right course.

A word of advice for parents and coaches: The greatest gift you can give a child is to teach her or him to know who they are, to recognize their authentic way of being, and to encourage them to express it. You are not fulfilling your greatest duty as a parent or coach if you only produce children or players who are made in the image of what you think is right. The best coaching and parenting brings out the best in another.

Doug DeCinces's manager may have been a good manager, but he was not a great one. If we look at the great ones—Vince Lombardi, Phil Jackson, and John Wooden—we find men who showed respect for their players. The last two coaches for the Super Bowl (2007)—Tony Dungy of the Colts and Lovie Smith of the Bears—both had a unique coaching style based upon respect, not intimidation. Coach Joe Taylor, four time Hall of Famer, has a great saying, "They don't care what you know until they know that you care."

This principle of individuation is very relevant to your survival when your life is falling apart. When a crisis hits, you are often forced to make very important decisions: life-changing decisions like, "Do I have surgery?" "Do I take the buyout?" "Do I sell my home?" "Do I stay in this marriage or separate?" These are some of the most challenging decisions you might face in your entire life. Typically, the answers must come from you and your choice is important. If you can make these choices from a depth of maturity and clarity without being influenced by external pressures, you will probably be on solid ground.

SELF-ANALYSIS—INDIVIDUATION

Answer the following questions: True or False

1. I generally tend to go along with the group.

2. I feel more comfortable when others accept me.

3. I like to fit in.

4. I do not spend time in introspection.

5. I am usually confused regarding my beliefs on important issues.

6. I am usually afraid to express my thoughts and feelings when others disagree.

7. I am not interested in understanding different points of view.

8. I cannot assert myself with strong-willed individuals.

9. I am afraid I will be rejected if I speak out.

10. I have not progressed beyond my early childhood conditioning.

11. I usually defer to those in authority.

12. I am afraid to be angry.

If you answered "true" to two or more of the above items, you may need to do some personal work in the area of individuation.

Directions for Corrections

If you have identified individuation as a potential roadblock to your capacity for high functioning, then create the following action plan:

1. Obtain a life coach to help you speed up your process for change.

2. Begin a daily introspection process in which you identify any psychological blocks to being your authentic self:

   a. Fear of retribution for speaking up.

   b. Fear of rejection.

   c. Fear of loss and abandonment.

   d. Any tendencies to idealize others.

   e. Any belief that you should defer to authority.

   f. Fear of success.

   g. Fear of failure.

   h. Early childhood programming that you should please others to the exclusion of attending to your own needs.

   i. Boundary confusion (an inability to establish clearly defined roles and expectations with others).

   j. Rigid thinking patterns based upon group norms or religious dogma.

   k. An unwillingness to admit mistakes, be vulnerable, and hold yourself accountable.

3. Prioritize the above issues and begin to systematically address them one at a time.

4. Keep a written diary of your daily progress.

5. Engage in self-healing processes, such as "Inner Child Work," to free you from early childhood wounds and parental conditioning.

6. Forgive all those who have ever harmed you.

7. Develop a daily meditative/contemplative practice that awakens your intuitive awareness.

8. Make a conscious decision to listen to your intuition and follow it! Begin small!

9. Use your meditative/contemplative practice to discover your life's purpose.

10. Begin each day by asking your higher power to guide and direct your life according to the divine plan.

11. Develop the courage and wisdom to speak the truth. Do not lie, avoid being in the moment, or avoid addressing what is happening right in front of you. Use your good judgment to know how and when to speak up.

12. Listen to your heart, trust yourself, and serve the highest good in each moment.

CHAPTER 6

THE SIXTH PRINCIPLE:

A DEPTH OF HEART WILL GIVE YOU THE DRIVE, DETERMINATION, AND INSPIRATION TO PERSEVERE

Success in life requires a passion and desire to succeed! You have to really love what you are doing. A big heart creates a dynamic driving force, which gets you out of bed in the morning and motivates you to do whatever it takes to succeed. Heart generates the drive to succeed. Your drive gets you to work harder, practice more, read more, become more educated, and train harder. If you sit home and wait for something to happen, it won't! Greatness cannot be achieved and sustained without a strong drive for success. Those who have a strong work ethic are more likely to achieve lasting success. Especially in difficult times, it is very helpful to stand out as the best and shine above others. When times are tough, it is especially important to "keep on keeping on" to overcome all obstacles. It is important to do whatever it takes to improve yourself, and that takes drive. It certainly helps if you love what you are doing. It is very difficult to have the inner drive to work hard if you really do not like what you are doing. When you know what you love, it is easier to follow your heart. If you love what you are doing, the drive and inspiration will be there to support you. This force cannot come from the mind or some idea of how you think you should be. Heart comes from the soul and the depth of your being. You cannot fake heart!

Heart makes you care about what is happening to you, your loved ones, and the world around you. Without heart, your life becomes dry, and your life begins to lose something. You may go through the motions, but without the drive and inspiration, you may not have the energy to get you through the tough times. Heart not only inspires you, but also inspires those around you to be their best.

Lee Brandon, the two-times Women's World Long Drive Champion, has a particularly compelling and inspiring story. It is very relevant to our discussion about heart. Lee had her arm severed in a near-fatal accident when she was in high school. Doctors told her she would never use her arm again and only reattached it at the insistence of her mother. Over seven years, Lee rehabilitated her arm and became a fitness coach and World Long Drive Champion. Her healing process was difficult and profound. We have a lot to learn from her. Let's hear in her own words what happened.

INTERVIEW--LEE BRANDON
THE ACCIDENT

I asked her, "When you were seventeen, you had an accident. How did the accident happen?"

"That was a near-fatal injury to my left arm. I was in the county playoff basketball game; I was in Long Island in New York. I had my head turned as I was walking through this locker room door that happened to have a pane of plain plate glass in it. I was talking to some friends and turned to walk through the door, and I fell through. It was like a guillotine; it basically came down out of the door facing. Where the glass was positioned—it was right where your hands would fall. So I fell through the glass, and that was it. I was in intensive care for ten days. They re-attached my left arm, and when I was in the operating room, the doctors basically said that my chances of waking up with an arm were less than 30 percent. So in my heart, as they were knocking me out under the anesthesia, I was trying to envision how I was going to play basketball with one arm, or how I was going to survive with one arm.

"It really was a life-and-death experience for me. It was the light at the end of the tunnel. I flat lined at one point, and they resuscitated me. And it was a radical blood infusion at the time, in '79. So it was a big deal."

I asked, "Did you have an out-of-body experience?"

"Oh, yeah. I was on the roof, looking back at myself. I was out of myself. I was looking back at me on the table. Everything was very far away, and all I could hear was people yelling at me, 'Breathe, breathe, breathe!' But it was like they were five miles away from me; I could barely hear them.

"And at one point I remember praying, because we had just gone through, in Bible study that week, the parable of the faith of a mustard seed. And that was pretty much it. I said, 'Well, if you have the faith of a mustard seed, it says you can move a whole mountain.' And so, in my little seventeen-year-old mind, I thought, 'Well, if I have the skin of the faith of a mustard seed, that's not a lot, a mustard seed is so itsy-bitsy and tiny, that I know for sure I have that much faith. And my arm's not as big as a mountain.' So I was trying to rationalize in my mind, as my breath was fading, that if I just believed, that I would wake up with an arm. And at that point in time, it almost felt like two hands came under my ribs. It was pretty intense. My out-of-body experience was where I felt like my lungs lifted. It felt like somebody grabbed my ribs and went, 'Pssshhwww!' And I went, 'Oooooh'—then I was able to breathe. And that was it, I came back. And so I survived the whole thing. They let me out of the hospital. It was seven years before I could use my hand again. I used it, but it was seven years before I was able to feel it again. So, it was pretty intense."

COMMENTARY

Lee's experience of her breath being pulled out of her is not unusual for those describing such experiences. In yoga literature, it is often described that the breath is sucked out of the lungs, and then awareness moves into another realm that is not identified with or located in the physical body. There is a state in meditation practice that is referred to as the "breathless state." In this state, the technique of "watching the breath" and learning to control the life force energy allows consciousness to become internalized, and the life force energy is withdrawn from the outer senses into the higher centers of the brain. As a consequence, breathing is slowed down, heart rate is slowed, and finally the breath stops. It is possible to exist in this state for hours without any physical damage.

The average person can use his or her sleep state to begin to observe this process. Upon gaining awareness in the morning as you awaken from sleep, pay attention to your breath. In the state just after dreaming and just before being fully awake, you may notice that your breath is very slow, and then an influx of air enters the lungs with an inhalation. This breath, which is linked to the life force energy, fills the lungs, and the consciousness is revived for normal wakefulness.

BACK TO THE INTERVIEW

I asked Lee Brandon, "While you were out of your body, did you have any kind of experience with a spiritual presence?"

"You know how people make pacts when they're under tremendous stress? Well, I think I felt very close to that great hand. Like, I felt like I was being held by something bigger than me. And the promise I made myself was that I would always find a way to give, and help the kids, because the only thing I could think of, laying there on my deathbed, was not necessarily my family, but camp, and the positive things, and the sports. I wanted to come back to be able to do that kind of work, and that's what I've pursued my whole life. I've stayed committed to that. I always wanted to go do workshops for kids. So I think feeling that help and feeling that support at that intense time, and knowing unequivocally that my life was saved for a reason, was how I've always lived my life.

"I've always believed against all odds that I would do something bigger than me, something that I was meant to do, and that I was alive for a reason. Even when I started competing at Long Drive—win, lose, or draw—I always felt like it was such a great opportunity, that I was just meant to be doing that. And that my comeback, and using that arm that I was given ... I couldn't have been doing that with one arm and be at that level, so I have always tried to press myself. And then people say, 'Well, if you haven't been golfing for a long time, you can't compete at that level.' I don't even listen to them, for the same reason I didn't think that I couldn't ever ride a unicycle. I just knew in my heart that if somebody else could do it, I could do it. So I've always had this set of expectations around my performance."

"When you came out of surgery, what state was your arm in?"

"It was in a partial cast; it was triple its size now. It was ready to explode. It looked like train tracks were on my arm, because the scar was so huge. The scar goes almost from my wrist all the way up into my armpit. And it still looks like a railroad track, but not as bad as it did, because it was so thick—it's about the size of my thumb. And the doctors always said I would have issues with the arm, but I'm like, 'Well, if it's there, I don't care.' It was tough. It healed at a right angle, so it took me years to try to straighten it and years to try to bend it, because it was frozen at this right angle."

I asked, "And how did you get it to straighten out? What did you do?"

"Well, from 1980 to '85, I spent years working on my own in the weight room, trying to just get the hand to work. I would have tennis balls. I would always be carrying something in it to try to make sure it could hold something. I invested many hours. I took piano in college, and I would have never taken piano. But I challenged myself by teaching myself guitar. And the guitar and the vibration of the strings, and the sound, made my hand start waking up. And after seven years of that kind of rudimentary biofeedback, I was actually able to have full sensation back into my hand. There are still parts of the arm and parts of the hand that are numb; but overall, it's nominal compared to what it was."

"Last time we got together, you told me a story about a guy who saw you in the weight room."

"Yes! I call it my 'Buddy Bob' story, the story of me and my buddy, Bob. I don't think the man even knew me or paid attention to me, but I always watched everything. I was sort of isolated because of my arm injury, and while all of my friends were out dating and out doing fun things, I was in my room trying to get my arm to work, or in the weight room trying to get it to straighten.

"I know what it's like to feel like a handicapped person, or to feel physically challenged, where you're not allowed to do things because of other people looking at you—inhibiting you. And I was forced to do certain things that were really against my grain, and going from being a competitive, high-end athlete, to going to a school where I had to scrub toilets to get myself through school, was really like eating humble pie for four whole years.

"I would walk down the hill in the morning going to work, and here was this lone silhouette on the track, walking around the track, hour after hour after hour. I would be sitting there eating breakfast, and I'd be looking out the window, watching this man walk around the track.

"Finally one day, after probably six months of seeing him, I started waving at him, and he'd wave back. And we created this long-distance kind of a mutual respect for each other. And then I started seeing him in the weight room, and he would see me fighting with my arm, trying to get it straight. And it must have been my junior year—he walked past me in the weight room when he said, 'Do you have any idea what I'm training for?'

"I said, 'No.'

"He goes, 'I invest hours of my day out on that track walking because I'm going to walk from California all the way to D.C. for the Veteran's Association.'

"And I'm like, 'Well, that's great. That's, like, unbelievable, because I know I see you there all the time.'

"He goes, 'Why are you crying?'

"Because I'd always go to the weight room and I would be sitting there, because basically in order to straighten my arm, I had to rip the scar tissue. And I said, 'Oh, my arm's just killing me, and the doctor's say I'll never be able to straighten it.'

"And he said, 'Don't listen to them. Don't listen to them. What does your heart tell you?'

"And I said, 'Well, my heart tells me I'm going to keep working it, and it's there, it's meant to do something other than what it's doing.'

"So he basically looked at me and he said, 'Just don't rob yourself. Don't rob yourself.'

"And I'm like, 'Whoa!' I wasn't quite sure what that meant then, in 1983.

"And it must have been 1987—I got a picture in the mail from my buddy Bob [Wieland]. I was in New York at the time, where I was an adjunct professor at Hofstra University, and I was working as a head strength coach at that university, running sixteen of their teams. So I was, like, a bigwig teacher/coach. I'd really shifted into a whole other gear, and I got this picture from him, and he basically said, 'This is what happens when you don't rob yourself.' And he had made it. It was a picture of him with President Reagan, and he was shaking hands with him. And it must have been 1989; I was running a program that I had pioneered that was a New York state-funded program, not-for-profit, with athletes against drugs. I was there with three of the top NFL football players from the New York Jets.

"I was standing in front of these kids telling them not to rob themselves, and telling them the story about my buddy Bob, and you could have heard a pin drop in the room when I said, 'He walked across the United States on his hands.' Here was a man who had lost both of his legs to a land mine, who was a Vietnam vet, and he walked across the country on his hands. So here was a man, in 1983, that looked at me, with two good arms—one that was sort of compromised and didn't quite work—but here was a man with no legs walking past me on his hands. He would plant his hands on the floor and then he'd swing his torso through. He had a specially designed saddle that he put on his stumps. And he would walk. Instead of using a wheelchair, he would just walk everywhere. He had arms the size of my thighs. He still holds records.

"I just got a call from him yesterday; he's going to go do some strength routine things at the Arnold Classic in Columbus. And he's still a very motivated and motivating character in my life. He's a great man. And basically I stood in front of those kids and I would tell them about my buddy Bob. Here was a man with no legs, telling me, with one arm, not to rob myself. You talk about changing my life. I felt like at some point it all came back to certain key people, and he was one of those key people that forced me to not feel sorry for myself—that if he could do it, I knew I could do it. I didn't know what I needed to do, but I knew I could do something other than just sit there and cry for myself. So by the time he shook president Reagan's hand, my arm was straight, and I was lifting, and I was running programs. I was the first woman to be hired in the NFL for a pro football team as an assistant strength coach, and since then I've been in the industry for many years. It's been nonstop, exciting … I haven't scrubbed a toilet since!"

Commentary

I was fortunate to meet Bob Wieland one day at Lee's gym. Lee was giving me some coaching on fitness training and Bob showed up at the end of our session. I was able to sit down and speak with him for about ten minutes. During our conversation, I was reflecting on how we often define ourselves based upon our physicality, especially in Southern California, next to Beverly Hills. Mr. Wieland has a very strong presence about him. He is very, very present. He looks you right in the eyes and gives you his full attention. There is a tangible energy that surrounds him. His sense of being is much stronger than the average individual. I was struck by the fact that this was a man who had half his body, but he was more present and more substantial than most people I know. It was certainly a great example that we are really much more than our physical bodies!

Back to the Interview

I asked Lee Brandon, "So would you say the power of the will has a lot to do with the capacity to succeed in life?"

"Yeah. I think it all comes back to—just to decisions. And when I was on my deathbed, I had two decisions: quit, or keep going. And I think we all face those decisions every single day. Give or not to give. Breathe, not breathe. Push, don't push. And at that point, I didn't see … I think, to me, if I think of the word 'will' or 'willful,' that doesn't always paint a powerful positive visual in my mind. But if I think I have the option right now to move or not to move, I have the option to breathe or not breathe, then there is no option."

Commentary

It is probably worth defining the "will" at this point. When Lee refers to the will or being willful, she is referring to a personality function that is more ego-centered. I am not using the term "will" within this context. At a personality level, we have all experienced people who seem very willful. This is not usually a positive state. This type of willfulness is often experienced as oppositional and rebellious. It comes from an effort in the personality to try and get what you want—like a two-year-old throwing a temper tantrum. That is only one type of will.

I was referring to another type of will—a will that is the result of a strong, focused intention. A strong will, from this point of view, can be the result of an inner, inspired passion that is highly focused to achieve a specific goal. A person with poor concentration, unclear goals, and poor self-discipline will not have a strong will. A strong inner knowledge of a sense of purpose and direction and a strong inner connection to some deep core results in a stronger will. Lee Brandon has all of this, even though she may not think of it in these terms.

Her strong will in association with her depth of heart produces tremendous drive. Can you imagine what it took to rehabilitate her arm over seven years? How many of us would have the sustained drive to accomplish such a feat? I believe that her profound inner spiritual connection created a sense of meaning and purpose that resulted in her life dedication to helping and serving others. She knows that you will always receive more than you give.

During times of distress and tragedy—physical, spiritual, emotional, or financial—you often need some depth of inner resource to give you the strength and drive to keep going—to keep making the choice for life and to master defeat and despair. This inner reserve is often the result of some connection to something greater than yourself. A mother's love for her child will often result in extraordinary actions in times of need. A commitment to a greater cause or a sense of connection to a great purpose will create inspiration and drive to work harder and achieve the seemingly impossible. An inspired heart is a powerful force that can move mountains, heal the physical body, and change nations. Lee's passion and desire for greatness is a tangible force that continues to help and inspire anyone who has the good fortune to be with her.

DIEGO CORRALES

It is very common in the boxing world to hear about heart. It is often said that the fighter has a great heart in the heat of battle. We can learn a lot from professional boxers. I was personally surprised to find them the most heart-centered of all the athletes I interviewed.

Our discussion about heart is in reference to finding the inner strength and drive to overcome adversity. Fear, pain, and doubt are inherent in difficult and challenging times. Having the heart to move through immense and potentially debilitating forces is essential to success. Diego Corrales shares some great insights on this subject.

INTERVIEW—ON PAIN AND FEAR

"Doubt, pain. Let me tell you. Pain is the biggest encourager of fear. So, if pain is the biggest encourager for fear, you have to learn how to deal with that in order to overcome fear. I think that the drive in those individuals, as well as myself, kind of pushes me past that point—the pain and the fear. There was no such thing. It just helps me move past it. These guys, you know, Michael Jordan was out there—twisted ankles, limping everywhere he goes, but he'll go out there and still shoot a thirty-five point game, and take his team up to that level. Serena can go out there and have the worst set, hurt herself, and still come back and beat anybody. That is the ability to just find ways. I mean, look at John Elway. I tell you what. The best I've ever seen. He breaks his pinky—breaks his pinky. And I think that was in the playoffs—the NFC playoffs. Maybe it was the Super Bowl. He breaks his pinky. And they show the thing, and his pinky's turned all sideways, and it's all jacked up. And they're in the playoffs, and he's— his desire is to be there and get these guys over the top. They go in back there, and they show him on the bench, and there are things that'll fix it, they crack it, and they tape it up—then he's going back in the game. They won that game. They were losing. They won that game. But that has to be, like, the biggest … I mean, when you see that— athletes, that's it, the compelling story is the drive. Go to the movies. All the stuff we see in the movies, you see in sports every time you go out there."

142

COMMENTARY

I find it interesting that my question was about doubt, but the conversation quickly became focused on pain and fear. Diego actually went to the deeper question, to the underlying dynamic; doubt is the result of fear and pain, and can be a prime element that creates fear. Fear of pain is common. It is more obvious in boxing, where someone is attempting to pound your face and knock your head off; it is not hard to find the source of pain there! However, people are afraid of all kinds of things because they create pain: loss of a loved one, loss of a child, loss of a job, loss of money, loss of pride—the list goes on and on. Some say there are only two things in life—love and fear. Fear takes us away from love. So the doubt may be whether we can avoid the pain. Are we too afraid to face the pain and deal head-on with the circumstance? Sometimes we think the pain will be more than we can tolerate. Lee Brandon certainly did not run away from her pain.

As human beings, we are very protective of what we have. We try to hold to what we believe—what we possess. Our ideas become possessions, our health becomes a possession, and our beauty becomes a possession. We can become so afraid to lose it all that we stop fully living. Life is risky. It takes a lot of courage to move into the situation that can cause pain. How much courage does it take to step into the ring and know you will be hit—and hit hard—time and time again? How much courage does it take to open your heart and tell the truth to your husband or wife when you know they may not like what you say and might chose to stop loving you? How much courage does it take to serve your country and place yourself in harm's way?

There is something noble about the human spirit. Like Diego said, "All the stuff we see in the movies, you see in sports every time you go out there."

That is why we love sports—because we get to see the greatest expression of the human experience. We get to see the drama of life unfold in a short, controlled episode. We see victory and defeat. We see the power of the human spirit to overcome adversity, to overcome fear, to battle through pain, and to come out the other side. This happens on the battlefield, but we are not there to see it. We just know that it is so. We all have our own battles to fight. Sports help inspire us to find the strength and courage to win our battles and stay in the game. The last US Open [2008] certainly had this drama with Tiger in so much pain with an injured knee, but still fighting to win.

Once again, Diego points to the fact that we must have that inner strength of character to overcome the fear and keep in the game. Where does that come from? Are we talking about the will? Diego seems to have found it as a child with the help of his father—strive for perfection and win at any cost. His time in prison seems to have also strengthened him, but he had it long before that. Prison probably just matured him and helped him to refine his development.

How do you overcome fear? Where does the strength come from? I do believe it has something to do with the will. The human will is a strong thing. It can move mountains. It is a force like no other. When the will is unified with the heart and soul, and directed by a clear mind, it can accomplish anything. For the sake of this discussion, let's call this "conscious directed willpower." The Secret speaks to this reality. It is the power of conscious willpower to create an energetic force that affects reality. Conscious directed willpower brings more energy into the body; it can heal disease in oneself and others and help manifest your life's dreams.

Conscious directed willpower requires a choice. Lee Brandon talked about this. We can "choose to breathe, to move, to act." I suggest we can choose to become 100 percent present and go deeper inside to access a hidden reserve of power. The doorway to this power is through the heart, not the mind. It is through the soul, not the ego. It is through transcending the little self into something bigger, not through selfishness.

Great athletes embody this force. They have a presence about them that is tangible to anyone who has the sensitivity to see. They are centered, balanced, and focused. They do not waste energy. Each movement seems to have purpose. This inner, dominating willpower is what makes champions. It is not the techniques they use, the equipment they have, or the clothes they wear. It is the depth of who they are—the nature of their Being that results in greatness. You can feel it standing next to Jim Brown or Tiger Woods. They have done the work and developed inner resolve to overcome adversity, to overcome pain, and to overcome doubt. The result is a force to be respected. It is Tiger fighting back to win the 2008 US Open in the midst of excruciating pain; it is Diego "Chico" Corrales getting up after being knocked down twice in the tenth round to deliver a technical knockout to José Castillo.

DIEGO ON DRIVE AND A STRONG WORK ETHIC

I asked Diego Corrales, "In my interviews with other athletes, like Jim Brown, they all say you really have to work hard and develop a skill level."

He answered, "The one thing that I really take pride in is how I work. I work, and I know I work harder than, I'd say, at least 90 percent of the boxing community right now. And I'd say I could maybe see one, two people working as hard or harder. It's very hard to work the way I work every day, at the pace I work every day. It's hard to do that. But I just somehow wake up every day looking to do it again."

COMMENTARY

I don't think we can talk too much about a strong work ethic or drive. Two of the greatest players on the PGA tour, Tiger Woods and Vijay Singh, both work very hard at their game. One of the potential problems with today's children is that they may have it too easy. Learning to work hard and put out one hundred percent effort is a character quality that is usually developed in childhood. Moreover, those who are really successful actually find joy in working hard and doing a job well. If a child is always resentful of having to do the work, then he or she will never internalize a strong work ethic that will last them a lifetime. The bottom line is that if you really want to be able to perform at your best, you have to prepare for it. You can't just think about it and hope that everything will line up when the moment counts. You have to prepare for success. Hard work and practice allow an individual to master basic mechanics so it becomes instinctive. It is only in this way that you can get your mind out of the equation and let your instinctual, intuitive, deeper self take over.

I asked Diego Corrales, "Any advice that you can share with young people, who are up against that wall and are struggling, that can help them find the inner strength and courage to overcome all that?"

BACK TO THE INTERVIEW WITH DIEGO

"Yeah. The one advice I can give to anybody going through that would be: just never know how to quit. If you quit, you'll never know what you could be. If you quit, you never know the possibilities that may come. So that's the thing. If you quit, you'll never know how far you can go. I would say, never leave the question, 'What if I would have…? What if I would have…?'

146

"Don't leave yourself with those questions. There are many people out there today that have the same questions. 'I could have been this, but I ...' or 'What if....? — I wonder if I could have ...?' There's no wall too high — there's nothing you can't grab if you drive for it, single-minded. Maybe you ought to make everything like a mission, single-minded—an objective, and go for it. That's it. That's my advice."

COMMENTARY

Diego offers great advice to anyone: "Never give up!" You will never know what you can accomplish if you don't give it all you can. Life will always test you. Some tests are more difficult than others. Certainly, going to prison is a tough one. There will be people who try to make you afraid and try to create doubt in your ability to succeed. Don't listen to them. They are part of the test. Don't take it personally; they are part of the cosmic drama, playing a role. In fact, they can make you stronger.

It takes a lot of mental strength to maintain a single-minded focus and accomplish a goal or fulfill a sense of purpose. Once again, the more deeply you are connected to your core sense of self, the more inner direction you will receive to discover your life's purpose. Remember, the pathway to your core self is your heart, not your mind. Each one of us has to find meaning in life which will inspire us to get out of bed each day and work as hard as we can to accomplish it.

Typically, inspiration comes from the soul and is a spiritual thing. When you feel connected to your deeper self and have a degree of spiritual realization, then you will find new strength, meaning, and energy to accomplish things. How you find that spiritual connection is your business.

There are many ways. You have to find the way that works best for you. But to be sure, you will always be tested, and if you give up, you will never succeed. Perseverance is one of the key elements to success. Any great success story is filled with times of defeat and temporary setbacks. You can successfully overcome any setbacks in your life if you keep connected to your heart, keep trying, learn from your mistakes, and readjust when necessary.

BACK TO THE INTERVIEW

When speaking to Diego Corrales, I said, "Boxing is different from most sports, because it is more serious. You can get seriously injured if you are not at your best. In golf, if you miss a shot, it goes in the wrong direction. It may cost you a lot of money, but it won't put your life at risk. If you are boxing and not at your best, there is real danger. Perhaps because of this real danger it brings out something more from these athletes."

He answered, "You win at any cost. You do what you have to do at any cost. And it was, like, pain was never the thought. We just did it all. Whatever it took—that means you do it to win. That's something that you've got to have inside of you … that every individual … the greatest athletes in the world all have that inside themselves, and no matter what it was—Michael Jordan, Troy Aikman, you look at the best, Venus and Serena, Tiger, whatever—they all have a common denominator, and that is, no matter what it is, no matter how it happened, no matter what injury they're going through, whatever mental image they're going through, whatever it is, they find a way to excel past the rest of the pack. Even when the rest of the pack is still close, they find a way. And that's something that's just inside. You just got to know how to take that—know how to plow through."

COMMENTARY

What is this elusive quality that allows an athlete to plow through? Perhaps it is that quality that we call heart. Heart is a combination of passion, drive, and a desire for excellence. It is the spark within that ignites the extra push and the extra effort. It is the energy that emerges in the bottom of the ninth, with two outs, bases loaded, a full count, when the team at bat is three runs down. It's the last pitch, and the hitter connects for a grand slam! It is that magic that propels Michael Phelps through the water in the last twenty-five meters in the breast stroke when he is half a body length behind and he hits the wall 0.01 of a second in front of the next swimmer to win yet another gold medal. Heart is the quality that keeps Tiger going hole after hole in the US Open in spite of the pain of a badly damaged knee and broken leg. The heart of a true champion never gives up!

Heart is not something that you learn from a technique. It is a reflection of character and a love for life. Perhaps you can inspire another to awaken heart, but you cannot give it to them. Heart is there, latent and ready to be awakened. It is something that each of us has to find for himself or herself. It is easy to see if someone has heart, but difficult to activate if it is dormant and asleep. The great players have it; the mediocre players need it.

Like many personal qualities, it is possible to develop certain traits if one has desire. Intention sets in motion the power and energies for change. If you really want something, set the intention to do whatever it takes to achieve your goals. If you want more heart in your life, set the intention, and pay attention to what happens in your life. You will be given the opportunity to develop that quality. Remember, however, that you really have to want it.

Heart becomes so important when we are confronted with a life crisis.

Those who have fought back from cancer have fought a real battle. Their effort and struggle reveals a depth of strength, courage, and determination. When I worked with terminally ill children, I was always moved and inspired by them. They had a light and presence around them that was tangible. Their love and radiance was something to behold. I always felt fortunate to be with them.

Back to the Interview with Diego

I asked Diego Corrales, "When you are fighting, have you ever felt anything from the inside that has given you some extra strength or inspiration to help you excel?"

He answered, "I remember, my best experience with that was—it was in a losing effort, too; I had been down, I'd been down for the first time—no, the second time. And I was like, 'Okay.' It was after the two years; I had been off for two years, and just now, my first big step back up again, getting myself back, knowing I'm not quite as sharp as I should be, trying to fight at this level."

"Casamayor fight?"

"Casamayor. And there was, like—you go down the first time, the second time, and I was like, 'Ah, come on.' And I remember, he was coming in, he was coming in. And I was like, 'There's no way. I've got this cut that's bleeding over my eye, but there's no way I'm going to lose, there's nobody going to beat me.'

"That's all I can remember thinking in that—as the referee's counting, that's all I can think. The drive just ... I mean, from that point, it was like, 'Let's go, hit the gas.' And that was, like, everything; the momentum shifted immediately, and that was probably one of the best feelings of it that I ever had. It was like, "Let's do it, let's do it now." Now, just—my body turned it on. I think that was more emotional than anything else, just I had to do it."

"They stopped it," I said. "You wanted to keep going."

"Yeah, they stopped it on a cut, a freaky-looking cut. Well, it was a freaky thing, period; and all through my lip, from the inside—oh, yeah, you could see my teeth. When I was talking, you could see my teeth. It was kind of neat." He laughed. "But I wanted to fight so bad, I was like, 'I don't care about it, I don't care.' I mean, I'm ready to go. I got hurt again after they had stopped him—okay, yeah, the blood is freaky-looking and bleeding all over the thing. Who cares? Let's fight; it's the fight. I mean, I love the bloodbath; I love the whole idea of a blood bath, let's do it. 'Let's do it.' "

COMMENTARY

You have hidden internal forces that can be activated by your will. This may be related to your spiritual nature, or whatever you want to call that which is greater than your mind and ego. We talked about conscious, directed willpower. Here we see it in action. Diego has been knocked down twice and badly hurt. Rather than crumble and dissolve in the center of the ring, he digs deep and finds some force within him to "hit the gas." Once again, the depth and power of his being and all that makes him Diego "Chico" Corrales is called into action. His inner reserve—which is the total sum of his training, determination to win at any cost, indomitable will, and personal depth— brings him back from the banks of defeat and gets him up off the canvas. If you are looking for an example of heart and drive, here it is!

It is worth noting for any young person reading this. Notice, he did not whine, complain, make excuses, and try to blame someone else for his struggles. Some people in leadership are presenting poor examples and not good role models. I hope you do not model after them. Great leadership inspires others, takes responsibility, remains accountable, and respects others. A great leader is not constantly trying to impress you with his or her greatness. Your personal power does not come at the expense of others!

SELF-ANALYSIS—HEART

Answer the following questions: True or False

1. I am passionate about my life.

2. I feel inspired to help others.

3. I have a lot of energy.

4. I never give up.

5. I know what is important to me.

6. I love to help others.

7. I know my life's purpose.

8. I have a passion for excellence.

9. I am grateful for all that I have achieved in life.

10. Sometimes I feel so much love I am almost moved to tears.

11. I value my integrity.

12. I believe it is important to be honest.

13. When the going gets rough, it's time to "step on the gas."

If you answered "false" to two or more of the above items, you may want to do some personal work in developing more heart.

Directions for Corrections

If you have identified a lack of heart as a potential roadblock to your capacity for high functioning, then create the following action plan:

1. Obtain a life coach to help you speed up your process for change.

2. Begin a daily meditation practice and ask to be shown your life's purpose.

3. Discover what you are passionate about.

4. Raise your energy level by getting more aerobic exercise and changing your diet.

5. Reach out to help others.

6. Commit to learning something new.

7. Keep a written diary of your daily progress.

8. Deepen your spiritual life by inviting God into your heart.

9. Consciously strive to be an instrument of God in your daily life.

CHAPTER 7

THE SEVENTH PRINCIPLE:

EMOTIONAL INTELLIGENCE WILL DETERMINE HOW EFFECTIVELY YOU CAN REACT AND RESPOND IN HIGHLY STRESSFUL CIRCUMSTANCES

Many of the individuals interviewed for this book referred to Mike Tyson as an example of someone who was very smart but was undermined by his lack of emotional control. Several individuals spoke about Mike Tyson being a very intelligent man, even though his professional career collapsed. In fact, those professional boxers and other athletes who knew Mike were very fond of him. They were sorry that his career got off track. The Mike Tyson story is another matter. My thoughts on emotional intelligence germinated from that discussion and thereby became included in this book as a separate chapter.

While none of the individuals interviewed ever directly spoke about emotional intelligence, their lives and accomplishments give tribute to this important domain. They exemplify what can be accomplished when both physical talent and emotional strength are integrated.

The first book, *Bouncing Back*, was written and published prior to Mr. Tyson's very successful live show, *Undisputed Truth*. He has turned his life around and has shown to be thoughtful, intelligent, funny and insightful. We can learn from him and see how emotional intelligence can be developed and how it can be affected by one's environment.

Many people may not have realized that Mike Tyson is an intelligent man. When most people think of Mike Tyson, they probably have images of him in prison or biting off an ear. These images do not inspire a vision of a man who is thoughtful and insightful. The impression is more of a raging bull out of control.

There is a big difference between intellectual intelligence and emotional intelligence. Being intellectually gifted obviously provides a great advantage in life. José Torres believed that boxing was really a match of intelligence and character—more than physical strength. He attributed Mohammad Ali's great success to his great intellect. However, being smart is not enough. We have seen very intelligent athletes like Dennis Rodman struggle as the result of emotional issues, in spite of his fine mind.

One can actually be mentally gifted but have such a low emotional intelligence that they do some pretty stupid things. Emotional intelligence is about being smart in how you manage your emotions. Some people think that in business you should not have any emotions. As long as you are breathing, that is probably not possible, unless you are Mr. Spock. We all have emotional reactions to various situations. It is what you do with them that makes the difference. Emotional intelligence is the result of several factors: the awareness of your feelings, the ability to express your feelings, the ability to contain your feelings, the ability to organize your feelings, and the ability to resolve your feelings. It is possible to be intellectually intelligent but not have an equal and corresponding emotional intelligence. Just because you have a good mind does not mean you have done any work on your emotional self. Emotional intelligence is something that can be developed and learned. If we left children alone and did not socialize them, we would have a bunch of wild kids running around without inner controls. If you do the work, you can be emotionally smart as well.

THE AWARENESS OF YOUR FEELINGS

Have you ever asked someone close to you how he or she feels about something, and the response is, "I don't know"? The first step in emotional intelligence is to know what you feel. Without the knowledge of what and how you feel, you are lost. You will act and react based upon unconscious forces without any power for self-direction. You will become the victim of life's circumstances and can be manipulated by anyone smart enough to know how to get you all worked up and play upon your emotions. According to those who knew Tyson, this is what happened when Don King began to manage him. Don King got Tyson into an emotionally agitated state, and Tyson began to lose his good sense. All the athletes spoke of fear and doubt and the power of those emotions to undermine success. Self-awareness provides a deeper look and insight into those mental elements that will undermine performance. Self-knowledge allows you to overcome these thoughts and emotions that could potentially inhibit your fullest expression and success.

Doug DeCinces' great success is largely due to his work with a psychologist who helped him resolve his early childhood conditioning regarding authority. He was able to bring those feelings into conscious awareness and then adapt to his current reality. He would have been unable to assert himself with his manager had those powerful emotional issues remained hidden within his psyche.

Jim Brown expressed the need to maintain a state of inner purity in order to fully express his gifts. His degree of intuitive insight and spiritual power are enhanced by his self-knowledge. He also changed his career from football to acting when he was at the height of his athletic performance. He was aware of his desires and had the clarity to act on them when opportunity presented itself.

Dick Fosbury made a slow and steady transformation into the Fosbury Flop. He knew what felt right for him. He was able to honor his inner knowledge, which was constantly reinforced by real life success.

Lee Brandon struggled back from death's door to become the two time Women's World Long Drive Champion. She intuitively knew that she could recover and provide some valuable service to others. This awareness sustained her and continues to inspire her.

THE ABILITY TO EXPRESS YOUR FEELINGS

Knowing what you feel is the beginning, but to be really emotionally smart, you need to know how to appropriately express those feelings. The expression of feelings allows people to develop intimacy and solve conflicts. It is impossible for someone to relate to you over time if they do not know how you feel. Many people act as if they expect other people to read their minds and emotions. It is not other people's responsibility to read your mind—that is left for psychics, and they usually get paid for the service. Emotionally healthy individuals express their feelings so they do not remain stuck in their gut—especially the ones like anger, fear, and resentment. You can make yourself physically sick if you do not know how to process your emotions.

Once again, Doug DeCinces provides a vivid example of this issue. He was under a tremendous amount of stress and pressure. His emotions were heated up and about to explode. He could have easily physically attacked his manager, Earl, on several occasions—but to his credit, he did not. He was able to use words and tell him what was happening. He was able to set limits and establish appropriate boundaries—"I am not playing second base anymore!!" He was able to effectively perceive reality—a policeman standing there—and contain himself.

This level of emotional integration and maturity stands in stark contrast to those players who totally lose control and explode with wild emotion and typically get themselves fined or expelled from games. We have seen players on the basketball court rioting with the fans or golf pros like John Daly turning to food, alcohol, and physical rage reactions because he does not have the emotional maturity to resolve his inner demons and effectively communicate what he feels and needs. We have seen politicians like Anthony Weiner ruin a career and a marriage because of inappropriate acting out and sending lewd texts.

Mike Tyson's rage reactions in the ring appear to be a function of frustration and anger and a total lack of personal emotional integration. He did well under the guidance of a loving, supportive trainer like Cus D'Amato, but for many years he was unable to sustain that level of performance on his own.

Diego Corrales died tragically in a motorcycle accident following a decline in his boxing career. The police report indicated that his alcohol level was elevated. I know that winning was very important to Diego, and he felt a great burden to be a positive role model. I suspect that his self-destructive behavior was the result of these inner conflicts that were not openly resolved. He was a wonderful man and I regret that his life came to a close in such a manner.

It is especially important in times of crisis to have the emotional maturity that allows you to acknowledge and appropriately express your feelings of loss, anger, and frustration. I have seen too many people get stuck in denial about financial loss, emotional problems, or life-threatening disease with the delusion that everything will magically disappear and get better. Unfortunately, things typically only get worse due to avoidance, poor decision-making, and inaction.

The Ability to Contain Your Feelings

Sometimes we have some pretty strong feelings—like wanting to bite someone's ear off or take an AR-15 or a Glock 17 and go shoot someone. However, an emotionally mature individual does not act on every impulse that arises. Just because you feel something does not make it appropriate to express it or act on it. If everyone went around expressing all his or her emotions, we would have a very chaotic society—just as if no one ever expressed how he or she felt, we would have a very repressed society. There is a balance. That is why we call it emotional intelligence—because you have to learn how to be smart about when to express what you feel. Sometimes when you have very strong feelings—whether they are very powerful loving ones or angry ones—you need to hold on to them and allow yourself to understand what is going on. Giving full vent in the heat of the moment is not always the best choice—getting upset and impulsively sending out a tweet at 3:00 am may not be the best way to handle hurt feelings. We see this loss of control in every aspect of life—sports, marriage, and international relations. We see individuals and groups engaged in riots, fights, brawls, war, and murder. These are good examples of pretty poor levels of emotional intelligence.

The Doug DeCinces story provides another good example for us. When his manager took him off the bases after hitting the double and replaced him with a slower runner, he did not fly off the handle and express his rage. He was able to keep it in. Sometimes we have to hold on until the appropriate time is available to discuss what is on our minds.

I had the privilege to speak with Ray Mancini, who held the World Boxing Association Lightweight Champion title for two years in the 1980s. On November 13, 1982, Mancini met twenty-three-year-old South Korean Duk Koo Kim and won by a knockout. Kim was severely injured and died a few days later in the hospital. Ray told me that was the most difficult challenge in his entire life. He was especially distressed when fans would approach him on the street and ask him, "Ray, what is it like to kill somebody?"

Ray was very hurt by these reactions. He did not go into a rage and make the situation worse. It was bad enough. He lost major endorsements for cereal companies because of the bad press and the poor image around such a tragic event. He actually called upon his spiritual life and found comfort and strength in prayer and his relationship with God. I asked Ray what helped him during this time. He answered, "My faith—power of prayer. I'm a firm believer of power of prayer. I'm a firm believer in that. Say your prayers. I'm a firm believer of the old saying—when there's trouble, be still, listen to your heart, it'll answer you."

There is no one specific way to correctly manage your inner life. Certainly, many people have found a spiritual relationship with God to be a powerful source of peace and comfort. The fact is that a real, tangible relationship with Spirit provides a sense of inner peace that transcends worldly problems. Even when your outer life may be in turmoil, it is still possible to find a quiet place within that allows you to remain focused, positive, and functional. Whatever your method, it is important to know how to access this positive inner realm.

Trey Waltke provides another good example of this principle. His claim to fame is beating Jimmy Connors in the Canadian Open and John McEnroe in the same year in 1983. I asked Trey, "What do you think was your greatest moment? What is your greatest success?"

INTERVIEW—TREY WALTKE

Trey explained, "Probably for me, personally, it was beating Jimmy Connors at the Canadian Open, because it was just as much a mental battle for me to get over, because he and I grew up playing at the same club in St. Louis. And even though I was the best eleven- or twelve-year-old, he was three years older than I was, so he was starting to conquer the world and everything else when he was young—you know, sixteen, seventeen. So I was always compared to him, and I used to play with his mother on Sundays, and he would play against my father when we were eleven and fourteen. So for me to finally beat the guy later on when he was #1 in the world, for me was a real mental battle as well.

"What I recall specifically, more than anything about the match, was that I was in my hotel, and I was getting ready for everything, and I went downstairs to take a taxi to the match. And we got stuck in a huge traffic jam. It was a big accident. And I'm looking at my watch, and I realize that I'm not going to make it. And there's nothing that I can do. So finally the traffic moves, and I remember telling the guy, 'Look. You have to literally pull up behind the stadium, and I'm going to have to jump the fence or talk to the guy. Just run on to the court. No checking—just go on the court.'

"So the whole stadium was there, waiting. And I ran onto the court. And

I remember thinking that I really had no time to over-think it. It was like someone threw me in the pool and I was on auto-pilot. I had the adrenaline going from being late, for one. So I wasn't nervous about playing; I was nervous about something else. So I used that sort of adrenaline, and I just kept on going on it, and I just got into a—as they call it, a zone of playing phenomenal the whole time. And that's what I recall about that match more than anything."

COMMENTARY

It would have been natural for anyone to be overwhelmed and totally lose focus at this point. Not only was he competing against his childhood opponent and #1 in the world, but also he was late, rushed, and had no time to warm up. It takes a strong character structure to keep focused and contain all the emerging, competing, and arising feelings. This is a very clear example of emotional maturity and strength that is part of emotional intelligence.

INTERVIEW—JOSÉ TORRES

During my interview with José Torres, we began to discuss Mike Tyson. I asked Mr. Torres, "What do you think happened with Mike that his career changed so dramatically?"

He answered, "Emotionally, he never had emotional control. And he needed to have a guy on top of him, someone on top of him that he respected, and when Cus D'Amato died, that was the end of Tyson. He was out of control. He was more emotion than anything else, because Tyson was such an intelligent guy, you know? I feel pity for him because he knows … you discuss boxing with him, and you'd know how smart he is. He's really amazing, how he loses control emotionally."

THE ABILITY TO ORGANIZE YOUR FEELINGS

- Set priorities.

- Develop goals.

- Have a clear direction and maintain focus.

- Develop a well-established set of values and principles.

Highly complicated situations are charged with intense emotions. It is easy to get confused and jump from one solution to another and become overly influenced by outer forces. It is imperative to have some inner guidance system to keep you on course and create priorities with clear, precise, obtainable goals. If inner emotional turmoil forces you to lose focus, you will be at a disadvantage and may flounder.

A clear set of well-defined values can be a guiding beacon during dark times. When you know who you are and what you believe in, then it is easier to stay on course. Life will test you. Your inner certitude and clarity will save you when the outer world appears most chaotic. It is during the most difficult times that you must draw upon your inner reserves. This is another important component of emotional intelligence.

For example, if you have lost a significant part of your personal wealth, you will be driven to your core values. Are you defined by what you own? Is your happiness determined by what you have? Is the meaning of your life determined by what you can buy? Hopefully the answer to these questions is no!

Currently, it is easy to get caught in fear. We have terrorist's threats and activity across the globe and here in America. Our sense of safety has been compromised. Many have lost jobs as business and manufacturing became more global. Police activity has been under scrutiny because some communities have found serious racial prejudice in law enforcement. Instant videos show Black people getting shot by law enforcement without justification. ISIS threatens the Middle East and is constantly attempting to disrupt Western culture. Individuals fall of the mental cliff and murder innocent people in movies theaters, schools, and churches. Climate change threatens to change our very way of life. With all these real threats to your security and peace of mind, do you go into reaction and let fear run your life? Do you become paranoid and see everyone who is different from you as the enemy? Do you want to withdraw, build a wall around you to feel safe? America is unique because we are built upon inclusion and integration. We are a melting pot for many cultures and provide a unique opportunity for a better life. It has been a long struggle, and we are clearly not there yet, to integrate people of color and women into every aspect of our society. These have been our values. What are your values and does fear for your comfort, security, control, and survival overwhelm you and throw you into a primitive reaction of fight or flight?

If your deeper values are grounded in love, service, community, and gratitude you might find the inner strength to remain on course and not let the fear, chaos, and uncertainty that confronts us all to take over and drive your actions. The sad truth is that too much fear creates separation and turns people against each other.

Oftentimes it is easier to define your core values when you are overwhelmed by the fear of loss. In the West, we believe that material gain will bring great happiness, but in fact, may only lead to more stuff without any real change in your inner life. Oftentimes a simpler life brings greater peace and joy.

However, adjusting to the demands of severe life changes is not always easy. It is usually accompanied by confusion, doubt, anxiety, and despair. We are witnessing massive destruction and death in Syria. Millions of people are being uprooted and becoming refugees. Countries and communities are being changed with the inflow of refugees. Many Americans fear this change and vow to resist it. Last night [January 28th, 2017] Austin, Texas Mayor Steve Adler gave a national TV interview and explained how his city has benefited from all its new citizens with no increase in violence. He views his community in very positive ways. Your values are being tested. Do you even know what you really believe? It is important to take some thoughtful time to introspect and search your heart. Find out who you really are and what you truly believe so you can keep your values, direction, and priorities clear when life tests you.

Competition in professional sports often provides us with great examples self-mastery or breakdown. Given the horrible things going on in the world today, murder, war, destruction, climate change, etc., sports may seem rather trite and trivial. However, we can learn from these stories and gain some inspiration and direction for self-mastery.

In the final holes of a major golf tournament, you are ahead by two strokes. Two great players are making a charge right behind you. This is your first chance to win a major tournament. Your mind is beginning to race— What if I win? My whole life is going to be great! What if I lose? I don't want to blow it! Should I lay up or go for the green in two? What will people think if I lay up?

There is a saying sports, "you need to learn how to win." This refers to your mental state. You have to learn to keep focus and stick with your plan. You have to stay strong and focus on your internal core values, priorities, and purpose. The movie, Tin Cup provides a great example of this learning process. Our hero, a talented golf pro who owns a run-down driving range, is on the final hole to win the Masters. This man has no discipline, and his emotions are out of control. He has no organizing principles other than to look good and demonstrate how great he is. He can win the tournament with an easy layup, but his ego compels him to go for the green in two. He puts twelve shots in the water before he makes a spectacular shot. He shows his talent, but blows the tournament. He wins the ego contest, but fails on the emotional intelligence scale.

When you are overwhelmed with lots of feelings, life's choices become more difficult. Life can also become very confusing. Another aspect of emotional intelligence is the ability to process all those feelings and put them into their proper place. Some thoughts and feelings need to be given high priority and addressed; others need to be ignored. It takes a well-integrated personality to process all these thoughts and feelings and come up with the best course of action. Great results don't happen by accident. If you have internal psychological problems with uncontrolled emotions, your life may be problematic, and crises and stress will probably overtax your ability to effectively cope. It might be wise to work on your inner life and raise your emotional integration so you will be better prepared when life's tests and struggles appear.

Lee Brandon is an excellent example of effective emotional intelligence. She was overwhelmed with emotion, grief, and fear when her arm was severed. She spent seven years in personal rehab to regain the function of her arm. She could have been lost and given up and frantically jumped from one healing method to another. She had a strong set of core values based upon her faith and her intuitive knowledge from her heart. When Bob asked her, "What does your heart tell you?" She replied, "That I am destined to do something important." She was able to devise a plan, contain her feelings, and keep her focus on the goal, regaining sensation and use of her arm. It took seven long years, but she was able to succeed.

John Daly, a very talented PGA Tour golf professional, provides us with an unfortunate example of someone who lacks in this important area. His values appear to be centered on avoiding personal discovery and development. His abuse of alcohol—like all those who go down that path—serves to cover up underlying problems. While it may not be fully conscious, his values appear to be based around avoidance of anxiety and distress and the externalization of blame and responsibility. His solutions create problems; they do not solve them.

The Ability to Resolve Your Feelings

Emotional intelligence requires an inner life that is free from long-standing emotional conflicts. If you are holding old hurts, fears, or resentments, then it is very difficult—if not impossible—to fully live in the present. It takes a lot of psychic energy to live fully in the present—to consciously be aware in each moment. If your energy is caught in the past, focusing on old issues, then you are less able to fully engage in life as it is. Resolving old, unfinished business is a must for anyone who wants to live a happy and peaceful life. It is impossible to perform at your best if you are stewing over past or future events.

Several years ago, I was speaking to one of the world champions in the men's RE/MAX Long Drive Competition. He had not won in a few years and wanted to get back on top. We explored his life, and he was concerned about his new family and his kids. He asked me if I thought those issues could distract from his ability to win again. I said yes and suggested he find a local therapist to help him with his family issues.

Recently I was watching some clips from the RE/MAX Long Drive event, and the announcer was discussing how this individual had been working with a sports psychologist and had, in fact, won again. Since he was a few years older, I don't believe that his physical strength had increased. I believe that his work on his family and emotional life had freed up his energy to perform at his highest capacity.

Lee Brandon, another RE/MAX Long Drive Champion, made great use of our time to help her rise above old emotional patterns that were triggered by the very vicious and catty verbal attacks she received from the other female competitors. Women generally have better verbal skills than men—and they can use that talent in very destructive ways. Our work together allowed Lee to become emotionally strong and unaffected by the comments from the other women in this competition. I was surprised at the high level of stress and anxiety that existed in this competition. I would watch women stand in the entry shoot, about to go to the tee for their turn to hit six balls. These players were so anxious they were just trying to keep from throwing up.

You can pay a high price if you do not resolve your early childhood issues. My interview with Diego Corrales revealed that he had a strong need to excel. His father, according to Diego, was a perfectionist, and Diego identified with that trait, as he had a very strong work ethic. He had high expectations for himself. He had made a notable comeback after serving fourteen months in prison for domestic violence. He said,

"I just put in my head that I wasn't going to let anybody see me fail again. And that's really how I do. It took some time, and it took some counseling just to make myself better and become a better person all the way around. And here I am, just driving every bit as hard as I started from when I first came back home—just can't let my family see me fail. Can't let anybody down, can't … I represent a lot of people, men that have hit that wall in life, and when that wall knocked them down, they didn't get back up. I'm the one that did."

His counseling helped him overcome some emotional problems, but it appears he did not go deep enough to resolve his concerns about letting people down. My intuitive sense is that Diego was deeply shaken by the loss to Joshua Clotty. His career never recovered after that. His death in a motorcycle accident involved alcohol. I know it must have been very difficult for him not to live up to his own standards.

On a more hopeful note, we see how much Doug DeCinces benefited from emotional awareness and personal development. He was able to stand up for his own rights and set the stage for a very successful life as a professional baseball player. He continues to be successful to this day as the owner and developer of Strawberry Farms Golf Club.

In summary, emotional intelligence is as important for success as any other quality we have discussed. When you master yourself, you increase the likelihood for success. You are a complex system and will probably not be your best if you remain unconscious and unaware. When you learn to manage your inner life, you can maximize your inner resources and learn to make better decisions and act with greater clarity, perception, and direction. Inner peace and clarity allow you to focus and get your mind out of the way so you can perform and function at your best. The need for emotional intelligence is even greater when life circumstances become unstable, economically challenging, or life-threatening. It is natural to feel fear, anger, and confusion during these difficult times. However, it is imperative that you resolve and manage your emotions so you can make good decisions about what to do and not let yourself become overwhelmed by fear or despair. If you can keep your energy positive, maintain peace of mind, and hold onto your values, then it becomes possible to hear your inner wisdom, make good decisions, and help solve problems.

EMOTIONAL INTELLIGENCE IN TODAY'S WORLD

Today we have a president that appears to have little emotional intelligence. His actions, speech, and thoughts appear to be over determined by the pressure of his inner life. His ego, oversensitivity to narcissistic wounds, and his need to be perceived as powerful and great appear to keep him focused on personal issues and continually create national drama and distraction by his false allegations. President Trump is a bully ready to pounce at the drop of a tweet—any perceived insult results in massive retaliation and infantile name calling.

In addition, his ability to process reality and integrate complex information appears to be questionable. It appears he actually believes in all the "alternative facts" he creates. It is too soon to know the consequences of his actions. However, it appears that the future will be pretty chaotic. Unfortunately, he presents a good case study for the importance of emotional intelligence in managing highly charged and complex situations. I hope my criticism of President Trump is not premature and too severe. However, since the stakes are so high, I feel the need to speak up. Let's hope the first week of his presidency settles down and we see more order, clarity, and a sense of inclusion for opposing views (a basic tenet of democracy) in the coming days. Unfortunately, there is nothing in President Trump's history to suggest that such a change is forthcoming.

SELF-ANALYSIS—EMOTIONAL INTELLIGENCE

Answer the following questions: True or False

1. I realize what I am feeling in specific situations.

2. When I become upset, I know why I am reacting.

3. I introspect daily to deepen my self-awareness.

4. If I have interpersonal conflicts, I am able to distinguish between my feelings and the feelings of others.

5. I am not quick to anger.

6. I am able to articulate my feelings to others.

7. I can describe my emotions with clarity.

8. In highly charged, complex situations, I am able to discern the various feelings and issues involved and take appropriate action.

9. I speak up when necessary.

10. I have clear and well-established values that guide my life.

11. I am able to define clear goals that guide my actions.

12. I am able to set priorities and adhere to them.

13. I am able to forgive others.

14. I am able to resolve old hurts.

15. I am able to let go of anger.

If you answered "false" to one or more of the above items, you may need to do some personal work in the area of emotional maturity.

DIRECTIONS FOR CORRECTIONS

If you have identified emotional maturity as a potential roadblock to your capacity for high functioning, then create the following action plan:

1. Obtain a life coach to help you speed up your process for change.

2. Begin a daily introspection process in which you identify what you are feeling each day.

3. Resolve old, underlying issues, such as:

    a. Anxiety

    b. Anger

    c. Fear of embarrassment.

    d. Fear of shame.

    e. An unwillingness to take responsibility for your actions.

4. Prioritize the above issues and begin to systematically address them one at a time.

5. Keep a written diary of your daily progress.

6. Develop a daily meditative/contemplative practice to deepen your self-awareness.

7. Begin each day by asking your higher power to help you become more emotionally mature.

Chapter 8

The Eighth Principle:

Openness to Personal Coaching Will Allow You to Rapidly Learn, Adapt, and Change

Successful individuals learn from others and learn from their mistakes. If you think you know everything or can succeed without the benefit of coaching, you are limiting your potential success. If you think you can do it all by yourself, you may be throwing away great resources that can speed up your learning. Being coachable simply means that you are open to new information and actively seek it out. If you are open to feedback and welcome the opportunity to realize any blind spots, then you are coachable. If you are closed to new ideas, new information, and personal feedback from others, then your door is closed to rapid learning and development. In highly competitive situations, this may cost you dearly.

The quickest way to learn something new is to ask an expert. You don't have to reinvent the wheel. Others have gone down your road before. If you have to prove something to yourself, such as your worth, value, and ability, then you might not consult others. While you will eventually feel more empowered if you go it alone, it might take you a lot longer to do so.

It is very difficult, if not impossible, to see yourself clearly without the benefit of a mirror. A good coach, teacher, or adviser offers you that mirror in order to speed up your progress and development. Knowing what the issues are for development is the biggest and most important part of change. You can't change what you don't know! This is especially true with regards to personal development. You might never see your blind spots without the help of others. Typically our closest relationships provide this service. If you find yourself bristling and resenting other people's personal feedback, then you appear to be closed to great opportunities for personal growth and development.

Coaching is also a tremendous help with regards to technical information. If you are exploring new areas in business, finance, or investing, you can avoid loss of time and money by consulting experts. One of the greatest coaching tools professionals use is to advise their clients to speak with an expert in his or her field. You can learn so much in a very short time.

You will hear from our athletes regarding the tremendous impact and value others contributed to their lives. There were often key people at a particular phase of their development, which helped them rise to the next level. You can also be helped by more subtle influences if you have the spiritual awareness. You do not have to live this life alone, separate and isolated from others and Spirit.

ON COACHING

First of all, I think it is important to understand that all coaching is not necessarily good. If you are going to trust your life and work to another, you need to get the best you can buy. Good coaching is designed to bring the best out of you. It is not designed to make you dependent. It is designed to make you more aware, help you to learn how to set goals, be accountable, stay focused, open your creativity and inspiration, and trust yourself. If you are getting technical information about specific processes and procedures, you want to be sure you have a real expert on your side. Everyone has opinions, but all opinions are not equal! A good coach should help you feel you can do your best. You should not feel humiliated and devalued. Of course, you can learn something from every experience, and sometimes you learn from your bad experiences. You become more empowered when you know when to walk away and have the courage to say no. Life and personal growth is complicated. You will be on solid ground if you look at every situation as an opportunity to learn. How you respond is the most important thing.

Secondly, coaching can address many different levels: physical, mental, emotional, and spiritual. The types of interventions a coach might make will probably vary depending upon the level that is being addressed. Not all coaching can feel warm and fuzzy. Sometimes you need to be confronted and if you have a big ego, that can hurt your feelings. It is important to know your coach, trust your coach, and know that he or she has your best interests at heart. Like Coach Taylor said, if you know your coach cares about you, then you will be more willing to listen and "take the coaching."

THOUGHTS FROM BUCK RODGERS

Buck had a very successful career in Major League baseball. We were talking about change and adjustment, and I asked him how he helped his players learn to adjust. I wanted to understand his approach to coaching. Buck offered this advice:

"I think it was just a matter of, you sit and talk to people and show them the way you think it should be done and say, 'What do you think about that? Does that make sense?'

"And I'll always say—whenever I wanted an answer, I'd say, 'I don't want you to say yes or no to this. This is what I think it's going to take for you to be successful. I don't want you to give me an answer right now. I want you to go home and think about it, and then you come in tomorrow morning and talk—but I don't want a reaction, I want a thought process to go through this, and see if you think you've got a better way to be successful, this way or that way. And then tomorrow, you come in and tell me your answer, and then we'll go from there.' "

COMMENTARY

Buck's simple process is really quite powerful. Too many times people try to change other people. They talk louder and longer, over and over again, hoping to wear the person down and by using the power of their will to influence and change another person. Personally, I find this style extremely obnoxious and totally ineffective. At best, you usually get someone to passively agree and then not comply with you later on down the line. At worst, you get a strong person who argues, resists, and fights back. What a tedious, useless waste of energy in this battle of egos!

Buck is an intelligent man who understands people. He knows that people have to want to change if something is really going to happen. Motivating a person to change is more of an art form than simply bullying someone into behaving differently. Transformation of character comes from the inside out, not from some external, coercive force. If you force someone to change, you will pay for it later. They will resent you, becoming openly hostile or passive-aggressive. You will certainly not generate loyalty and respect from that approach.

Buck is also skillful here because he does not ask for a response in the moment. Most people tend to react to external situations from an emotional perspective. A knee-jerk emotional reaction is usually not the most enlightened response. Buck helps to keep the situation more low-key by creating a space where his players can go home and think it over. He gives them the opportunity to consider his proposal and asks for their input—a sign of respect.

If you are coaching players or raising children, you first need to open the mind before change can happen. If you learn how to approach someone and facilitate a process that opens the mind to other possibilities, then you have made a great start in the change process. Everything starts in the mind. If you can engage the intellect and create an interest in the realm of possibilities, then you have the skill to be a successful change agent. A coach or parent is a teacher, and a great teacher helps others to open their minds and experience new levels of success.

Buck is a really solid guy with a down-to-earth approach. Here are some of his thoughts that are worth sharing.

Back to the Interview with Buck

"I've always felt that anybody that hasn't played athletics of some kind is missing something because of the competition. I love athletics; I think they're great for everybody. I'm sorry that in California schools you have to pay for your own stuff, and they aren't as accessible as they used to be. I think they are just as important in education as Latin or something like that. I think that we lack a lot of common sense in what we do—in our programs, our lawmaking, our coaching, whatever. Common sense is starting to become a lost art. And it's something that we see every day. A kid the other day gets suspended for doing a cartwheel outside gymnastics class. I mean, to me, they ought to suspend the person who suspended them. What's up with those kind of people? Those are the dangerous people—the people that can't understand the kids or the situations. Those are the dangerous people, not the kid that got suspended for two days that's eleven years old or whatever she is. Those are the things that you got to watch out for—people in high places without common sense, or sense at all. Those are the dangerous people in our society."

Commentary

It is important to keep your power and trust yourself, because you are the one living your life, and you are the one who will have to live with the results. Choosing to work with a coach does not mean you should become mindless! Remember what Jim Brown mentioned in his interview. You need to understand who you are and respect that. Know who you are and play to your strengths!

You also have to use your good common sense in a coaching relationship. I was working with a life coach a number of years ago when I was starting a new career in business coaching. I had the opportunity to go the New Orleans on a development mission with a large commercial investor. He wanted to give something back to the community, and he wanted me to help him. He offered to pay my expenses, but not anything else for this first trip. My coach told me I should charge for my time. I presented that to this man, and he walked away. I regret that to this day. It was an expensive lesson for me.

THE POWER OF SPIRIT IN COACHING

Great coaches have some special quality about them. It is not just what they know—it is also a question of who they are. The term presence refers to an unseen but very tangible quality of an individual. Bob Weiland, Lee Brandon's friend, has it. Martin Luther King had it. Dianna Ross had it. Paramahansa Yogananda, the founder of Self Realization Fellowship had it. Coach Joe Taylor has it. It is that feeling you get from someone that moves you to be better and uplifts your spirit. Those who have discovered the nature of presence understand this. Those who have been touched by others and felt their positive influence may not understand it, but do not deny its transforming effect.

If you are seeking a coach, look for someone who has developed a conscious state of presence. Jim Brown's experiences that we discussed in previous chapters are relevant here as well. His quality of being and his ability to "share his goodness" are a particular kind of coaching that goes well beyond the mind. It is the integration of one's spiritual nature in everyday life. This kind of coaching is rare to find.

This type of coaching is priceless. It is beyond the mind, outside of time, and it facilitates change at a very deep level. If you are conscious about your own spiritual nature, look for someone who has these gifts. They will understand you at a deeper level, and you will get more out of the relationship.

Those of you who think coaching is a waste of time or think that nobody really has anything to offer are misunderstanding the potential in a coaching relationship. A great coach has an intuitive power to perceive things in you that you do not know. He or she has the gift to energetically transfer something to you that can change your life. This can happen in an instant! On a more down-to-earth level, good coaching will help you focus, stay accountable, and obtain stated goals in a timely manner. It will also uncover any hidden blocks you may have to achieving your best.

Even accomplished athletes do not always understand the usefulness of good coaching. I was standing in the Nike trailer at the Nissan Open a few years ago with Lee Brandon. I began a conversation with a young man standing inside. He turned out to be Kevin, Rory Sabatini's caddie. He asked me if I worked with couples. He said he would talk to Rory and get back to me. A week later, he called and told me Rory does not believe in sport psychology—he was not interested. I think Rory missed a great opportunity to learn something.

Coaching can occur in a variety of ways. It can be a one-time contact or an ongoing relationship. It can be a formal relationship in which you pay for it, or it can be a gift in the moment when someone shows up to offer some insight that might change your perspective and your life.

Bob Weiland was an extraordinary coach for Lee Brandon. His comment, "Don't rob yourself," changed her life and the lives of many others through her. He was there in the moment and spoke up. The power of those few words stays with her to this day!

José Torres, the great fighter, gives us another example of the power of coaching. José was in the Army and training for the Army championship. He met Pasquale "Pat" Nappy who had a profound and life-long impact on him. José shared his story.

INTERVIEW—JOSÉ TORRES

"I met a guy by the name of Pat Nappy—Pasquale Nappy—and he was a wonderful teacher—you know, boxing."

I asked, "What do you think made him such a good teacher for you?"

"He began to talk about the mind, about thinking when I was there, and he was the first trainer that showed me that boxing was more a contest of the mind—more than the body. He was the first one that I understood that to be strong was okay, and to be fast was okay, but it was not the main thing. To possess those qualities is okay, but what you have to learn is to apply those qualities—the obligation of the possessor. And I learned that with him."

COMMENTARY

This is a very interesting choice of words—"the obligation of the possessor." I like this concept, because it states that to have talent is a gift, and you have an obligation as the bearer of that gift to manage and develop it in some way. The obligation naturally suggests hard work in developing the knowledge for applying those gifts. Learning the application takes the process to a higher level—to greater self-awareness and self-mastery. A good coach can help guide you to this end.

Mr. Torres suggests here that it is not sufficient just to have raw talent. It is great to have that, but to be a real champion, one must develop, mature, and learn how to use that talent.

Other champions that I have interviewed have also discussed the importance of hard work and refining one's skill. A good work ethic is necessary to be successful in any endeavor. The sooner a young athlete learns to appreciate the value of practice and training, the sooner they will be on the road to success. Once again, a coach can help guide you on the path that is right for you and help you obtain new insights that are relevant to your goals.

Within the golf world, it is not uncommon to hear someone express his or her desire to play better. When I ask them if they practice, they often say, "No." At first this shocked me, but now I take it a little more gracefully. However, I always think, "What do you expect? How can you get any better if you don't practice?" This is really in the realm of wishful thinking. "I wish I could be better without having to do anything." I don't know of any great achievements that were built upon a foundation of wishful thinking. The minister at my local Church had a very funny point to make on this very subject. He said, "You know, it takes a long time to accomplish something that you never work at!"

BACK TO THE JOSÉ TORRES STORY

I asked, "And how did he teach that to you?"

"Just by saying that the thing is, 'You have to learn when is the time to throw the punches. The timing is important.' I understood it right away. 'The timing and accuracy,' he says. And I thought that he was a genius when he said that. I knew that … I had an unconscious knowledge of that, and he was the first one to just bring it into the obvious. And I thought that he was a genius. And I admire him so much, and I stuck with him."

"And I'm curious about what you've said with regards to the mind," I said, "because I believe what you're saying is that the mind is everything, and that the body follows what the mind is able to imagine."

He answered, "I understood that right away—even though, like I told you, it was like an unconscious thing for me. I was looking to understand that. I didn't understand until he told me."

COMMENTARY

Here is another fabulous example of a life being changed by great coaching. Nappy did not try to control José or make him over in his own image. Nappy awakened some deep knowing within Mr. Torres that opened his mind and turned on a light that resulted in a world-class life. José's opening to Nappy is worth noting. What if José Torres had a chip on his shoulder and felt no one had anything to offer him? He certainly would not have had the lifelong benefit of friendship, wisdom, and support of Pat Nappy!

Another obvious example of the power of coaching is the Doug DeCinces story. As you may remember, Doug went to see a psychologist, a rather sophisticated form of coaching, long before it was in vogue to do so. Through that professional relationship, he was able to realize early childhood patterns that kept him from speaking up and setting appropriate boundaries with his manager, who had really been riding him hard. It was through his ability to assert himself at a very difficult time that he was able to create a long and successful career in professional baseball.

SUMMARY

The importance of coaching is undeniable. If you are too proud to admit that you need help, then you are cutting yourself off from valuable resources that can change your life. I have attempted to give you glimpses of the potential in coaching. You have heard some stories from some of the world's best athletes regarding their impact on others and how others have helped them. I encourage you to explore this important process in your life.

SELF-ANALYSIS—COACHING

Answer the following questions: True or False

1. I actively seek feedback on my performance.

2. I know I do not have all the answers.

3. I am committed to being the best I can be.

4. I would rather do things on my own than seek advice from others.

5. I am comfortable revealing my weaknesses to those I trust.

6. I feel that people will take advantage of me if they know my vulnerabilities.

7. I feel very hurt if others do not approve of me.

8. I get angry when others suggest that I might have a problem.

9. I am fine—it is others who have the problem.

10. I like to collaborate with others.

11. I want the sole credit for my success.

12. I know as much as everybody else.

13. I am confused about how to take my life to the next level.

14. I seem to be stuck in a rut.

15. I am not as successful as I want to be.

16. I feel lost and confused.

If you answered "true" to one or more of statements 4, 6, 7, 8, 9, 11, 12, 13, 14, 15, or 16, you might consider exploring a coaching relationship.. Or, if you answered "false" to one or more of statements 1, 2, 3, 5, or 10, coaching might be a good experience for you.

DIRECTIONS FOR CORRECTIONS

If you have identified coaching as a potential roadblock to your capacity for high functioning, then create the following action plan:

1. Get over yourself and ask for help.

Chapter 9

Summary

We have covered a lot of ground, and we have been able to get a glimpse into the lives of a few great athletes. Our Eight Fundamental Principles are each important in their own right, yet there is an interconnection between them—each one is a pillar and serves the other. When all are present, the whole becomes much greater than any of the individual parts.

The stories and life experiences of these exceptional individuals confirm what I have come to know after forty years of work as a psychologist, consultant, coach, and spiritual teacher. An integrated life, combining a strong spiritual foundation with a healthy personality and adaptive psychological capacity, leads to a happy and productive life. I personally have found meaning and purpose in serving others. I have had significant successes, learned from my mistakes, and have been able to recover from extreme difficulties and setbacks. A spiritual foundation has provided me with a deeper wisdom and understanding of life's challenges and given me the inner strength to persevere, even when life has become very difficult.

On November 15, 2008, I received a letter from my major investment company stating that they were going out of business and would default on my first trust deeds. They mismanaged funds—perhaps to a criminal degree—and left me with very distressed property that was a cash drain, not an asset. I had lost all my income and needed to recreate my life. I am not alone. Millions of people have done the same thing. As I mentioned in the introduction, this is one of the motivating factors that led to the first book. The past few years have added new problems along with financial strain: extreme Islamic terrorism and the election of Donald Trump. This new book is my attempt to update the information so it clearly applies to our current needs and concerns.

I know these principles work. I have used them in my life, and we have heard various stories from well-known sports figures on how they have employed these principles as well. I now live in Phoenix, Arizona, have used these Eight Principles to see me through economic and physical recovery for disc surgery.

The lessons and wisdom shared by our athletes are neither abstract nor ethereal. The stories are real and down-to-earth. Some of these athletes have bled in the ring or in hospitals, and all have persevered to obtain noteworthy life achievements. None were handed a silver spoon in life, and all appear to be stronger and wiser as a result of their passion, hard work, and desire to fulfill a sense of purpose and follow their hearts' inspiration. I believe in the truth of their stories and the power of these principles to guide and direct our lives. I have used them in my own life and have witnessed thousands of people find strength and meaning from them.

Of the Eight Principles, spiritual awareness lays a foundation for the successful application of the others. Spiritual awareness implies that you have experienced something greater than yourself that embraces the universe. This greater presence is known to be comforting and supportive. It may take different forms, but the essential factor is that it is loving, wise, and powerful. When you are embraced by this presence, you feel safe, comforted, and protected. You come to learn that there may be a difference between your personal plan for success and happiness and the divine plan.

When you learn how to let go of your mind's limited ideas and willingly accept a bigger, more expanded view of life, the process of surrendering your ego and learning to align with your higher self or soul becomes possible, yielding a greater sense of peace and serenity. This process of letting go actually allows for a greater abundance of love, joy, friendship, and well-being. A real and tangible relationship with Spirit allows for a deeper sense of trust in life. The big picture begins to emerge from your limited, clouded vision of life to include a deeper understanding of your purpose and how you can learn from your trials and tribulations. Life's successes are not only measured by material gains, but also by your increase in virtues such as patience, compassion, wisdom, and love. Inner peace is the result of letting go, not from the successful acquisition of greater financial wealth.

When you are able to attune your will with the Divine will, then life gathers a different momentum. You are guided and directed to new and different people, places, and experiences, which then yield greater rewards than you had previously conceived. The phrase, "Seek ye first the kingdom of God, and all things shall be added unto you," is a road map for success. This is not an easy road, nor a road without tests and challenges—it is a warrior's path.

The benefit of a spiritual life or path is that it supports the development and implementation of the other principles as well. The spiritual principle is not sufficient by itself, but it will facilitate the development of all the others as well. I will show how they all work together.

Second Principle

Believe in Yourself and Open Doors to Great Possibilities

Belief in yourself is an important thing. Jim Brown's comments are worth remembering— preparation and practice are important foundations for a solid belief in your ability to perform. In order to trust yourself, you need to feel a sense of competency that is the result of proven success. If you work hard and prepare for the moment, then you will know you have an ability to successfully perform under stress.

However, there is a deeper aspect to this truth, as well. Jim Brown is a mystic who senses an inner ability to influence those around him. He speaks of transferring his goodness to others. He is referring to consciousness and energy that is more subtle than the observable physical, material reality. He has a conscious connection to a deeper aspect of his being that has the power to create good. These subtle qualities come from the soul. When you have realized this inner reality, you have a stronger belief in yourself, because you know you can accomplish great things. This hidden power is a spiritual power that can move across time and space and help to improve the lives of others and draw to you, through the magnetic power of the soul, necessary people and experiences that will help bring you success. Your understanding of yourself takes on a much deeper meaning when you have realized the subtle power that lies within your soul.

A spiritual practice can result in the direct realization of the soul. Once this awareness is achieved, then your belief in the Self is real and true faith is developed because it is based upon direct experience. It is not a mental function, imagination, or hallucination. It is the awakening of consciousness that permeates every aspect of your being.

Jim Brown spoke about being pure in order to access this state. It is necessary to do the psychological work to resolve emotional conflicts in order to keep the mind healthy and strong. Resolving emotional issues creates an inner calm and allows for a depth in meditation—a technology for soul realization. Your work will reveal a deeper, clearer, more authentic state of being that will give you greater confidence in your ability to succeed in life and help others. Your belief in yourself will be based upon a deeper knowledge of your full potential and not just ideas from your mind, wishful thinking, or references to past worldly successes.

Third Principle

Develop A Positive State of Mind to Exponentially Increase the Probability of Achieving Your Goals

A positive mind state is critical for success. Doubt and negativity will undermine and destroy your creativity and passion for life. You will become depressed, lifeless, and unmotivated when you doubt whether anything positive will result from your actions. Paramahansa Yogananda said, "Environment is stronger than willpower!" You will be wise to surround yourself with positive people and uplifting experiences. It is very difficult not to be adversely affected when you have prolonged contact with negative people and influences.

Jim Brown, Lee Brandon, Doug DeCinces, and others have said doubt is a very destructive force. Your positive mental state keeps your will and energy strong. Remember the studies done with thought and water crystals by Dr. Emoto. What you believe affects your chemistry and your health.

Once again, a strong spiritual life serves to support your ability to keep your mind positive. The nature of Spirit is loving, supportive, and hopeful. The presence of Spirit is uplifting and joyful. Worldly influences and forces can be a drag on your consciousness. The world is filled with fear, doubt, and negativity. "The end of the world is coming," according to some. Remember the fear propagated by the end of the Mayan calendar in 2012? The trailer for the movie 2012 is enough to create an anxiety attack! People continue to fight, create conflict, and kill each other. In addition, there are always those who say, "You will never succeed at that!"

Spiritual forces uplift you, encourage you, and inspire you to serve others and be your best. Deep meditation becomes like a shower of light that dispels the darkness in your mind. The peace that results from deep meditation and communion with Spirit calms the emotions and restores the body to health. A strong, positive mental outlook will keep you young and healthy. Meditation is the best anti-aging technique I know. A positive mental state will also keep you open to new ideas and new inspiration for tackling life's challenges. Lee Brandon's positive mental outlook brought her back from death's door to be a world champion and inspiration to millions. When your life is falling apart and you have not yet been recreated, it is especially important to stay positive, calm, and open to guidance and direction from within. There are millions of people in the Middle East struggling with this right now.

Fourth Principle

Your Ability to Adjust Allows You to Adapt to New and Changing Realities

Your ability to adjust to new and changing situations is vital. If you get stuck doing the same thing, you will become obsolete and antiquated. If you cannot change, you will be very troubled in difficult times.

Change is synonymous with non-attachment. Sometimes it is necessary to be able to let go. If you are holding on, you may not be able to adjust to new circumstances. A strong spiritual life teaches you how to let go by transforming your identification with your mind, your body, and your emotions. As you let go of your ego identity, you will discover a deeper, more expanded sense of self. The process of non-attachment allows you to change without all the anxiety—especially when you deepen your trust in life's process and accept what comes in the moment. Successful spiritual practice creates mental flexibility, a necessary component for adjustment. You will be able to change more easily and without all the emotional drama that often is associated with letting go. When you trust that life is unfolding as it should and have the deeper awareness of intuitive guidance, then adjusting to new situations becomes much more graceful.

FIFTH PRINCIPLE

RISE ABOVE YOUR CONDITIONING AND SOCIETAL PRESSURES TO UNLEASH YOUR PERSONAL POWER

Individuation becomes more possible when you orient yourself to an inner source of guidance rather than the conventional ideas and opinions of collective society. Your true, essential self is a spark of the Divine and can be realized and recognized, but you have to develop the introspective sensitivity and ability to perceive this. The words, "be still and know that I am God," suggest that you will learn more when you quiet your mind and learn to listen to your inner life. Your soul provides a source of knowledge and direction that can guide you. Life can be complicated and some important decisions are difficult to make when they may have far-reaching consequences. Individuation requires that you rise above your childhood conditioning, have the strength to emerge from societal pressures, develop clear vision, and find the courage to speak up. This is an aspect of real authenticity: strength can be fostered and nurtured from a realized Self and a healthy psychological core.

Authenticity is a critical component of individuation. Authenticity has psychological and spiritual components—emotional clarity along with spiritual realization lead to higher levels of individuation. Each one of us has an authentic self that resonates in truth. There is a special ring and sense of power in the voice of the authentic self. Merely paraphrasing what others have said does not yield the same results. It takes solid psychological and spiritual work to realize your core authentic self and develop the courage to express it. However, the rewards for doing so are great.

SIXTH PRINCIPLE

A DEPTH OF HEART WILL GIVE YOU THE DRIVE, DETERMINATION, AND INSPIRATION TO PERSEVERE

It is very difficult to have the inner drive to work hard if you really do not like what you are doing. It is so much easier to follow your heart when you know you are doing what you love. If you love what you are doing, the drive and inspiration will be there to support you. This force cannot come from the mind or some idea regarding how you think you should be. Heart comes from the soul and the depth of your being. Heart brings passion to life and is ignited by inspiration. When the Divine touches you and you feel in harmony with the Divine will, then life becomes very meaningful and directed.

SEVENTH PRINCIPLE

EMOTIONAL INTELLIGENCE WILL DETERMINE HOW EFFECTIVELY YOU CAN REACT AND RESPOND IN HIGHLY STRESSFUL CIRCUMSTANCES

Emotional intelligence is the result of several factors: the awareness of your feelings, the ability to express your feelings, the ability to contain your feelings, the ability to organize your feelings, and the ability to resolve your feelings. It is possible to be intellectually smart but not necessarily emotionally intelligent. Just because you are intellectually brilliant does not guarantee you have learned how to effectively manage your emotional life. Your emotional life is a specific aspect of your being, just like your body is different from you mind. Just because you are smart does not mean you are in good physical shape. You have to work at it. Oftentimes emotional development is overlooked at the expense of other areas such as mental, physical, or even spiritual ones. However, if you have a strong spiritual life and want to work on your emotional development, you are ahead of the game.

A mature spiritual life results in the realization that you are not your emotions. You develop an ability to observe your experience and to not always be swept away by your thoughts and feelings. You develop a more consistent, solid core that allows you to "be with" intense situations and not be overwhelmed by them. You become a master of your inner life and thereby have more control to respond wisely. Since non-attachment is a foundation of spiritual development, it is easier to resolve emotional issues, because you are not rigidly caught or identified with them. You can realize issues and more easily let them go.

It is important to learn how to integrate your emotional life. You can lose connection to your heart when you distance yourself from your emotions. If you deny and avoid dealing with your emotions, you will most likely unconsciously act them out, which creates problems with others and undermines your effectiveness in critical situations. The value of a deep spiritual life is that it gives you added resources to work on your emotional health and progress more rapidly.

These various qualities have many levels. You can embrace them at a mental or psychological level and find value, direction, and enhanced competency in life. You can also look deeper into these qualities and find doorways for great spiritual openings and direction. As always, you will get as much out of this exploration as you put in. When you nurture your inner life, you will find the clarity, strength, and courage to survive your darkest hour.

I leave you with Jim Brown's thought: "If we were pure enough, we could probably fly."

EIGHTH PRINCIPLE

PERSONAL COACHING WILL ALLOW YOU TO RAPIDLY LEARN, ADAPT, AND CHANGE

Coachability refers to your willingness to be open and receptive to new ideas, experiences, and information. Coaching requires a degree of curiosity and interest in personal development. It requires a commitment of time and energy. It demands a degree of humility that acknowledges that no matter how intelligent you are, you might be able to learn something more.

Most often, the coaching relationship is an interpersonal one. You find a person who has knowledge and expertise in helping others. You form a relationship and work together as long as there is value. It is a long tradition for those who are successful to have coaches or mentors who have contributed to their success.

While this coaching process can be very successful when approached from a mental and psychological level, there are deeper avenues that are available when you are open to the inner wisdom and direction from Spirit. When you invite the Divine into your life, you will receive valuable and priceless guidance and direction. The more you sincerely open your heart and mind, the more your will receive. Remember, you are never alone. There is a great resource for wisdom and guidance within you. However, remember that God works through people. It is impossible to separate the hand of God from those around you.

CHAPTER 10

TOOLS FOR CHANGE

Change is not always easy. It takes commitment, self-reflection, perseverance, and determination. Sometimes change can happen in an instant. Other times it may take awhile. With each principle, I have provided some suggestions regarding "direction for correction." The final chapter provides more detailed suggestions and methods for personal development. There is a lot of information presented in this book. If you do 10 percent of the suggested methods and techniques, your life will change. The most important determining factor in change is your sincere, dedicated intent to change. Once you have made that decision, you will begin to see the process and opportunities unfold.

MEDITATION

Meditation has been suggested as a useful technique to use to deepen your inner life and develop a greater sense of peace, concentration, focus, and wisdom. It is the technique that will reveal direct access to your deeper Self and a personal relationship with God. Albert Einstein said, "The true value of a human being is determined primarily by the measure and the sense in which he has attained liberation from the self."

Meditation is not a state that you can make yourself be in. It is actually a process of learning how to let go. The mind cannot control the mind. Your ability to concentrate is like a muscle that must be developed. Fortunately, there are several yogic techniques that are proven to help you achieve deep states of meditation.

Meditation actually begins when you have internalized your life force energy away from the outer senses of taste, touch, sound, sight, and smell. The breath is actually the vehicle that controls the life force energy. The techniques that focus upon the breath and visualize currents of energy moving up and down the spine are very powerful tools to achieve this aim.

Once your consciousness is internalized and you have developed the ability to maintain deep concentration, you will discover an inner world of light, sound, smell, and energy that is very peaceful, loving, and joyful. This is the state of meditation. These techniques are tools to help you shift consciousness to your deeper self. Meditation is not a means to an end. It is both the means and the end.

MINDFUL AWARENESS TRAINING

Mindful Awareness is a common and simple meditation practice that you may find useful. To begin, simply observe the breath, which will shift your identification of self away from the ever-changing contents of your mind to the consciousness of awareness. You become the observer. The technique is quite simple.

- Sit either on the floor or on a chair with your spine erect, shoulders relaxed, and the chin parallel to the floor.
- Close your eyes and keep your gaze up through the center of your forehead.
- Breathe from the diaphragm.

- Allow your body to breathe on its own. Do not attempt to control the quality of the breath.
- Breathe through your nostrils.
- Place your attention on the sensation of the breath as it comes in and out of the body.
- Simply observe the breath. If your awareness moves off the breath into thoughts, images, daydreams, etc., simply return your attention to the breath.
- Continue this practice as long as you like.

This practice creates a fundamental shift in your state of being that allows you to become grounded in your deeper self, which is not identified with the mind. A figure-ground reversal will occur as the thoughts of your mind become the object of observation—you become identified with conscious awareness itself, which is observing the transitory thoughts and images of your mind. Your true or essential self will be experienced as stable, peaceful, joyful, and free from the effects of thought. If you want to learn how to do Mindful Meditation, you can find an MP3 download on my website at ronmann.com.

Mantra Meditation

Another way to deepen your meditation experience is to use a mantra (repetition of a word or phrase), which becomes useful, because it allows you to focus upon a single-pointed object—in this case, a sacred sound that carries a vibration of holiness. The single-minded focus becomes another tool to increase your capacity for concentration.

Mantra is based upon the theory that certain languages such as Sanskrit and Hebrew are "seed" languages, and as such, the sound of the word carries a vibration that actually changes consciousness. Therefore, mentally repeating a sound actually creates an inner vibration that transmutes consciousness into a higher state.

One example of a mantra is "so hum". It means, "I am that." Other mantras might be "om guru," "ram, ram, ram," "I am love," etc.

There is an ancient Tibetan chant, "om mani padme hum," that I personally like very much. It has been chanted for thousands of years, and therefore has great spiritual power. The words om (the cosmic sound of creation), mani (lotus), and padme (jewel) have a powerful impact on consciousness. As we have discussed, certain sounds carry specific vibrations. This chant is one of them.

Mantra Technique:
- Synchronize your breath with the sound.
- As the breath comes in, mentally repeat the first syllable of the mantra.
- As the breath goes out, mentally repeat the second part of the mantra.

Various Sanskrit mantras hold this power to fix the awareness on the sound and thoughts of the divine.

As one develops the capacity to stay focused upon the breath and the mantra, then the distracting thoughts of the mind recede into the background of consciousness. This process allows you to observe the contents of your mind and the field of emotions that come and go across your screen of awareness. This practice deepens your awareness that you are not the body, mind, or emotions. You become more stabilized as the observer and experience yourself as pure consciousness.

This practice develops an inner strength that is laser-like in its focus. Deep concentration and the internalization of your life force energy result in the direct experience of the subtle aspects of spiritual consciousness—peace, joy, and love. In addition, as you become calmer, you may be able to gain access to your intuition, which can help guide you through difficult times.

Carl Jung, the great psychologist, understood the power of gaining access to your inner life when he said, "Your vision will become clear only when you look into your heart ... who looks outside, dreams. Who looks inside, awakens."

The Self Realization Fellowship, founded by Paramahansa Yogananda, offers complete training in advanced meditation techniques. The highest technique is Kriya Yoga. It uses the breath and visualizations in the spine to deepen your capacity to internalize the life force energy and speed up your spiritual progress. You can learn more about these techniques by reading The *Autobiography of a Yogi* and signup for the lessons by visiting their website at www.yogananda-srf.org/. Kriya Yoga is the most powerful meditation practice that I have found. You might find it helpful as well.

You can also find meditation training in CD and mp3 form at my website: www.ronmann.com. Take a look at Inspiration for Meditation. It is a 30 minute guided meditation that will help you learn how to concentrate on the energy in the chakra system.

Another resource is my CD or MP3 download of the mantra, Om Mani Padme Hum in chanting form. This has been very popular over the years. There is the sound of the Tambura (classical Indian four string instrument) in the background that helps to create a meditative mood.

INTROSPECTION

It is imperative that you know what you feel and what you believe. If you are confused and lack personal clarity, it is very difficult to make important, life-changing decisions. In addition, it is important to have personal clarity about your thoughts and emotions in order to effectively communicate. Your ability to clearly articulate your thoughts, feelings, needs, and desires will dramatically improve your ability to manifest. You cannot do this successfully if you are lost in a confused inner fog.

This is what will help you:

1.   Spend time on a regular basis with the goal of achieving personal awareness of your thoughts and feelings. Many feelings begin with a physical sensation. You may not know what you are feeling, but you do feel something in your body. You may feel tension, tightness, contraction, or heaviness. Use your newly learned skill of concentration to focus upon the physical sensation, and allow information to come to you. It may come as a thought, image, or sense of knowing. Whatever it is, just allow the information to come to you. Be patient. Use your breath, breathe into the sensation, and let the information come to you. If you have repressed emotional memories, this can be a powerful process. If you become anxious or are too overwhelmed by what you are uncovering, contact a psychotherapist and get some professional support.

2.   Use a diary to write down whatever comes to mind. Do not think about what you are writing. Just allow a stream of consciousness to emerge. Writing engages a different part of your brain, and you might find that new insights and information become available.

3.   As you are about to fall asleep, tell yourself that you are going to have

a dream that will give you clarity about any issue on which you are working. Allow your subconscious to work in your dreams to help you. When you wake up, write down what you remember about your dreams.

AFFIRMATIONS—THE POWER OF THE SPOKEN WORD

Consciousness acquires power from the truth. All sacred texts explain that one gains the power to manifest what is spoken if one utters the truth. Our thoughts, when verbalized, carry an extra power. It is very destructive for us to verbalize fear, doubt, and self-depreciating remarks. During the most difficult of times, it is easy to regress back into mental and emotional states of fear, doubt, and negativity. It is most important to stay positive during these trials and tests.

Affirmations function to create a reality through the spoken word. For example, when work is slow, it is better to verbally affirm, "I am surrounded by wealth and continued work, and prosperity flows to me with great abundance" than to say, "I am screwed, I will never make it through this ordeal!"

You can implant positive thoughts into your subconscious mind by verbally and mentally repeating a phrase. Keep repeating the phase over and over again to solidify this deeper impression and positive thought pattern.

Here are a few examples of affirmations:
- I am calm and focused in the face of adversity.
- The universe will provide me with everything I need to support myself and my family.
- I surrender to the will of God, because I know Divine Mother has my highest good at heart.

Please create an affirmation that will support you at this point in time. Use it every day.

_____

_____

_____

PRAYER

Prayer is very powerful, because it invokes the presence of God. When you pray with devotion, you enhance the power of your spiritual practice. God has given us free will, and when you direct your love to God, it becomes a strong force to draw God's response.

Let's face it—during difficult times, we need all the help we can get. Remember that God created this universe, and you are a child of God. You deserve the help! You have to do your part and work hard, but through God's grace, doors can open, and opportunities can emerge that will help you. You might wonder, how do I know my prayers are working? The most obvious feedback is your daily life. Pay attention to what is happening every day. Also, when you are in a deep state of prayer, look for a sense of peace that will comfort you. This is a sign that your divine connection is real.

LEARN TO SURRENDER

Learning to surrender may be one of the most difficult challenges for us all. It takes a lot of faith and trust in the perfection of the divine order to not panic when things get really rough. It is a talent to make lemonade out of lemons. It is easy to say every difficulty has a silver lining and all challenges are opportunities for growth when life is good. It is more difficult to stay calm, optimistic, positive, and hopeful when your personal world is crumbling around you.

My own experience is that life is very forgiving. As the saying goes, "God giveth, and God taketh away." I have seen great losses in my life, and I have seen the resurrection as well. Never give up or lose hope! Keep on persevering, and you will succeed.

How can you learn to surrender? Acceptance and faith can be developed through time and experience. You need to learn that letting go and accepting what comes to you can lead to great personal growth, peace of mind, and unconditional love. You never know where life will take you. Each step on the path leads to new people, new connections, and new opportunities. One bad turn may take you down a path that leads to a pot of gold. Your mind cannot conceive or predict the unknown future.

Given this reality, I encourage you to try this: Pick a day and use it as an experiment. Make a consciousness choice to view everything that happens to you in that day as the direct will of God, and do not resist, react with anger, or attempt to avoid what comes to you. Stay in the moment and appropriately respond to everything. Be alert and awake and see how things go. If you make it through that day, try it on day two. Keep going until this becomes your attitude about all life's experiences. Remember, sometimes it takes a little time to see the wisdom and perfection of the universe. Be patient.

Personal Action Plan

The following section was created to help you integrate the information from this book into your life. Your final success will be measured by how you integrate the information into your life. I have created a thoughtful process to help you.

You have **strengths and weaknesses**. It is important to embrace both!

Please list your three major strengths:

1. _____

2. _____

3. _____

Please list your three major aspects that need improvement:

1. _____

2. _____

3. _____

COMMITMENT TO CHANGE

Please list three specific qualities or behaviors that you plan to improve in the next year:

1. _____

2. _____

3. _____

Please identify the benefits you will obtain from making the above improvements:

1. _____

2. _____

3. _____

Please list the consequences to you in both your professional and personal life if you do not improve in the areas listed above:

1. _____

2. _____

3. _____

POTENTIAL ROADBLOCKS TO CHANGE

Given what I know about myself, the following factors could keep me from accomplishing my goals for change and development:

1. _____

2. _____

3. _____

Action Plan

I plan to take the following actions to change in the areas I have chosen:

1. _____

2. _____

3. _____

Personal Support System

I recognize that I can be more successful with change when I make my intentions clear to another person and ask them to hold me accountable. **I plan to enlist the support of the following people in my personal action plan:**

1. _____

2. _____

3. _____

My request from each person will be:

1. _____

2. _____

3. _____

TIMETABLE FOR CHANGE

I plan to make the following changes in three months:

1. _____

2. _____

3. _____

I plan to make the following changes in six months:

1. _____

2. _____

3. _____

I plan to make the following changes in nine months:

1. _____

2. _____

3. _____

I will regard my action plan successful if I achieve the following:

1. _____

2. _____

3. _____

Good luck. I am available for individual coaching if you want some help. You may contact me through my website: www.ronmann.com or e-mail me at mannr@ronmann.com

Appendix

Contributors

The great Wisdom Teachings advise us, "Difficult times hold the seeds for great opportunities," "The true depth of one's character is revealed in the light of day," and "God's grace transcends worldly karma." These eternal truths can provide solace and direction during our current troubled times. Even though the outer world is in turmoil, your inner life does not have to parallel these pandemic problems. As the saying goes, "when the going gets tough, the tough get going!" You do not have to feel helpless and lost. There is a roadmap that will guide you through this maze of disorder. Others have struggled through tremendous adversity and have emerged victorious! You can learn from their stories and become inspired and gain the wisdom to make better decisions, adjust to the current demands of reality, and find your way through to better times.

I was fortunate to interview several unique individuals from the sports world. I spoke with people across various sports: baseball, golf, boxing, tennis, and football. Each person has a unique story, which reveals profound truths for personal mastery and survival during the most difficult of times. Sports are great because they contain the microcosm of life. We see all of our challenges, test, frailties, strengths, and successes revealed. Their stories reveal eight essential truths for self-mastery and victory in the most difficult and challenging circumstances. Let's meet these individuals who were generous enough to share their stories.

JIM BROWN

Jim Brown is the greatest football player of all time. He is a massive man of six foot two and has biceps the size of my calves. Aside from his tremendous physical strength, he has a presence that tells you not to fool around. One look from his eyes could stop a raging bull running at full speed!

James Nathaniel "Jim" Brown (born February 17, 1936) is an American former professional football player who has also made his mark as an actor and social activist. He is best known for his exceptional and record-setting nine-year career as a running back for the NFL Cleveland Browns from 1957 to 1965. In 2002, The Sporting News named him as the greatest professional football player ever.

COLLEGE CAREER

1954 - 1956. As a sophomore at Syracuse University, Brown was the second leading rusher on the team. As a junior, he rushed for 666 yards (5.2 per carry). In his senior year, Brown was a unanimous first-team All-American. He finished 5th in the Heisman Trophy voting, and set school records for highest rush average (6.2) and most rushing touchdowns (6). He ran for 986 yards—third most in the country despite Syracuse playing only eight games—and scored 14 touchdowns. In the regular-season finale, a 61–7 rout of Colgate; he rushed for 197 yards, scored six touchdowns and kicked seven extra points for 43 points (another school record). Then in the Cotton

Bowl, he rushed for 132 yards, scored three touchdowns and kicked three extra points. But a blocked extra point after Syracuse's third touchdown was the difference as TCU won 28-27. Brown is a member of The Pigskin Club Of Washington, D.C. National Intercollegiate All-American Football Players Honor Roll.

Perhaps more impressive was his success as a multi-sport athlete. In addition to his football accomplishments, he excelled in basketball, track, and especially lacrosse. As a sophomore, he was the second leading scorer for the basketball team (15 ppg), and earned a letter on the track team. His junior year, he averaged 11.3 points in basketball, and was named a second-team All-American in lacrosse. His senior year, he was named a first-team All-American in lacrosse (43 goals in 10 games to rank second in scoring nationally).

PROFESSIONAL CAREER

Brown was taken in the first round of the 1956 draft by the Cleveland Browns. He departed as the NFL record holder for both single-season (1,863 in 1963) and career rushing (12,312 yards), as well as the all-time leader in rushing touchdowns (106), total touchdowns (126), and all-purpose yards (15,549). He was the first player ever to reach the 100-rushing-touchdowns milestone, and only a few others have done so since, despite the league's expansion to a 16-game season in 1978 (Brown's first four seasons were only 12 games, and his last five were 14 games). Brown also set a record by reaching the 100-touchdown milestone in only 93 games, which stood until LaDainian Tomlinson reached it in 89 games during the 2006 season. Brown holds the record for total seasons leading the NFL in all-purpose yards (5: 1958–1961, 1964), and is the only rusher in NFL history to average over 100 yards per game for a career. Brown was also a superb receiver out of the backfield, catching 262 passes for 2,499 yards and 20 touchdowns. Every season he played, Brown was voted into the Pro Bowl, and he left the league in style by scoring three touchdowns in his final Pro Bowl game. Perhaps the most amazing feat is that Jim Brown accomplished these records despite never playing past 29 years of age.

Brown's 1,863 rushing yards in the 1963 season remain a Cleveland franchise record. It is currently the oldest franchise record for rushing yards out of all 32 NFL teams. While others have compiled more prodigious statistics, when viewing Brown's standing in the game his style of running must be considered along with statistical measures. He was very difficult to tackle (shown by his leading 5.2 yards per carry), often requiring more than one person to bring him down.

Brown retired, at age thirty, far ahead of the second-leading rusher and remains the league's eighth all-time leading rusher, and is still the Cleveland Browns all-time leading rusher.

In the 1960s, Brown helped form the Negro Industrial Economic Union to assist black-owned businesses. In 1988, he created the Amer-I-Can program, an effort to turn gang members from destructive to productive members of society. It is successfully operating in twelve U.S. cities and promoting a skills curriculum that is designed to teach inmates how to empower themselves to turn their lives around with positive self-esteem and self-determination. Brown helped to create a cease-fire between two of Los Angeles' most violent rival gangs, the Bloods and Crips.

ACTING CAREER

Brown had begun his career as an actor with an appearance in the film

Rio Conchos in 1964, then played a villain in a 1967 episode of *I Spy* called "Cops and Robbers", went on to star in the 1967 war movie *The Dirty Dozen* (during the filming of which he announced his retirement from professional football), the 1970 movie *...tick...tick...tick...*, as well as in numerous other features. In 1969, Brown starred in 100 Rifles with Burt Reynolds and Raquel Welch. The film was one of the first to feature an interracial love scene. Raquel Welch reflects on the scene in Spike Lee's Jim Brown: All-American. Brown acted with Fred Williamson in films such as 1974's *Three the Hard Way*, 1975's *Take a Hard Ride*, 1982's *One Down, Two to Go*, 1996's *Original Gangstas* and 2002's *On the Edge*. He also guest-starred in a handful of television episodes of various programs with Williamson. In 1998, he provided the voice of Butch Meathook in *Small Soldiers*. Perhaps Brown's most memorable roles were as Robert Jefferson in *The Dirty Dozen*, and in *Keenen Ivory Wayans'* 1988 comedy *I'm Gonna Git You Sucka*. Brown also acted in 1987's *The Running Man*, an adaptation of a Stephen King story, as *Fireball*. He played a coach in *Any Given Sunday* and also appeared in *Sucker Free City* and *Mars Attacks!* Brown appeared in some TV shows including *Knight Rider* in the season 3 premiere episode *Knight of the Drones*.

Biographical text courtesy of Wikipedia

I met Jim Brown at the nineteen19th hole of MountainGate Country Club. As I was walking in after a round of golf, I saw one of my best golf buddies, Don Dyer, sitting with a small group of black men. This was not unusual, since Don is a very well respected African-American who donates a lot of his time for the Urban League. Don is one of the finest men I know at MountainGate and has a heart of pure gold. I walked over to say hello to Don. He greeted me and said, "You should interview Jim for your book." I looked down and saw a very large and powerful black man sitting with Don, and to be honest, I had no idea who he was. A few weeks later Jim would say to me, "You don't know who I am!" But I am getting ahead of myself, and we will get to that part later on.

Not wanting to appear stupid and being bright enough to keep my mouth shut, I sat down and said, "That would be great." We all began to talk a little, and I kept looking at Jim. It began to dawn upon me that this must be Jim Brown. Sure enough, here I was, sitting and talking with the greatest football player of all time.

Don said to Jim, "You should play golf with Ron; he's good, he plays to a five."

Jim said, "Sure, I'll play you. I am a twelve, and I won't take any strokes, and I will beat you!"

"Are you sure you want to do that?" I asked.

"Yes, I am," answered Jim.

"Okay," I said.

A few weeks later, I happened to see Jim on the tenth tee. He asked if I wanted to play and suggested a little bet. I had a chronic lower back problem from two herniated discs as the result of a marital arts injury when I was doing Jujitsu fifteen years ago. On this particular day, my back hurt a little, so I said, "My back is a little sore. How about if we bet when I am feeling better?"

"Your back is a little sore?"

"Yeah, that's right."

"Okay, we'll just play for fun. We'll just have a friendly game."

So we teed off, and I hit a decent drive down the middle, hit my second shot on the green, and had two putts for a par. I was not paying too much attention to Jim's game, but I think he pared that hole.

Jim Brown is a big man. He walks like he has arthritis, undoubtedly from being hit so many times on the football field. In spite of his stiff body, he managed to hit the ball well and get around the course. I made par the next hole, and on the third tee, Jim said, "Let's just play for $5.00. Nothing much. You seem all right."

I was thinking that five bucks was not a big deal, and he seemed to want to bet, so I thought, what the hell; why not? So the bet was on. Now remember, Jim told me he was a twelve index, so he should have been making some bogies along the way. I was having a decent day and shooting even par as we went. Well, guess what—my newfound friend, twelve-handicap Jim Brown, was right there with me at even par.

We both bogeyed the par four sixth hole to remain tied, and we were on the tee at the 185 par three, seventh hole. I hit a good four-rescue to the center of the green. Jim pulled his tee shot way left and was in the rough, left of the cart path. At this point, I was thinking, I have him on this one. Well, Jim hit a great flop shot a couple feet from the pin and made his putt for his par. I missed the birdie putt, and we were still tied. As we were walking off the green, I jokingly say to Jim, "I thought I had you on this one."

Jim quickly replied, and he was not joking. "You don't know who I am!" He was not amused.

I thought, Oh, shit, now I am in trouble. The last thing I want to do is piss off Jim Brown.

The next hole was a long par four about 410 yards into the wind. We both made par on that hole, and we were still tied. I was one over with one hole to play. Jim Brown had kept an even pace with me on every hole—not bad for a twelve! It was a good thing I did not give him strokes; he didn't need any.

The ninth hole on the south course is a weird five-par—a dogleg left around a mountain. The entire fairway slopes to the right, and even a great shot will roll off the fairway unless you really keep it on the left side. It is rated as one of the worst holes in California. The club will redesign this hole when they decide to spend the money.

Jim and I were tied at this point. We both hit good drives and good second shots, leaving us about 130 yards to the pin. Jim was starting to rush a little because he had an interview with ESPN, and he was running late. He rushed his approach shot, came up short, and played out for a bogie so he could get to his interview. He jumped into his cart and drove away. I hit the green and two-putted for my par. I won by one stroke. I know the only reason I won was because Jim was rushing. If you even have the chance to play with Jim Brown, don't give him any strokes. I don't know what his handicap is, but this man can play golf!

DOUG DECINCES

Doug DeCinces was kind enough to grant me an interview at his office in Strawberry Farms Golf Course. Doug DeCinces now runs a successful real estate firm and has developed the Strawberry Farm course. He had a very successful career in Major League Baseball. He played for the Baltimore Orioles form 1973 to 1981 and was then traded to the California Angels, with whom he played until retiring in 1987.

Mr. DeCinces was a right-handed infielder who played third base. He was born and raised in Southern California and played Little League baseball in the San Fernando Valley.

Over his fifteen-year career, he hit 237 home runs; played in the 1979 World Series, in which he hit a home run in the opening game; played on the 1983 All-Star Team; and was elected to the Angels's All-Time Team in 2000. During his successful career, he won the American League Silver Slugger Award in 1982; hit twenty home runs in the 1978, 1982, 1984, 1985, and 1986 seasons; and hit thirty home runs in 1982. He also founded and sponsors the Doug DeCinces March of Dimes Celebrity Golf Tournament.

Doug DeCinces is a very intelligent and articulate man. He was generous with his time and his spirit. Although he is a very busy and successful businessman, we spent well over an hour in a very open and relaxed atmosphere at Strawberry Hills Golf Course, which he developed and owns.

All too often, we hear that it's a small world. Well, yes it is! Doug DeCinces and I were discussing childhood baseball and discovered we may have played against each other when we were around ten years old. I played on a local team in Santa Monica, and he was on a team in Northridge. This early childhood connection opened the way for a heartfelt, informative interview on professional baseball, coaching kids, steroids, and self-trust. While my baseball career peaked in Pony League with a pitching record of fourteen wins and no loses, he went on to become a great professional player.

While the stats Doug DeCinces has are noteworthy, the most powerful aspect of his professional career began when he replaced Brooks Robinson at third base. This is a great story that Doug shares with us.

Lee Brandon

Lee Brandon has lived her life defying the odds—from surviving a near-fatal accident that rendered her left arm completely useless, to becoming the first woman ever hired by the NFL as an Assistant Strength Coach for the New York Jets, to winning the 2003 Women's World Long Driver Invitational Championship Safeway Classic as well as winning the RE/MAX 2001 World Long Drive Championship in her rookie year having never hit a long ball in her life until the spring of 2001! Born in Muskogee, Oklahoma, Brandon moved with her family to Brentwood, New York at an early age. She became active in local, county, state, and national athletic events all throughout her school years. Long hours of tutoring paid off when in 1980, she graduated Brentwood High School in the top 12 percent of her class.

Brandon then went on to attend Ambassador College in Pasadena, California on an academic scholarship after countless scholarships had been lost as a result of her arm injury. During her four years, she trained and studied under Dr. Harry Schneider, US Olympic Track and Field Coach and traveled to Australia, New Zealand, Scotland, South Africa, and parts of the US as a motivational speaker/guest activities instructor for International Youth Camps. In 1984, she graduated as Vice President of the Ambassador's Women's Club and Most Outstanding Athlete with a Bachelor of Arts degree—with distinction. Returning to New York, Brandon became the Strength and Conditioning Specialist at Adelphi and Hofstra Universities on Long Island. While at Hofstra, she pursued her post-graduate work and was an adjunct professor, teaching thousands of students and athletes how to "Live Drug-Free, Lift Safe, and Stay Motivated." She also ran her own consulting business, where she founded "Athletes Against Drugs" and spoke at countless junior high and high schools with NY State funding. In addition, she consulted in health clubs in the New York metro area, where she designed and structured the One-on-One training programs. In June of 1990, the New York Jets brought her on board as the first female Assistant Strength Coach.

Lee has invented a unique and revolutionary system of strength and core training that is known as AB-Vanced NEU-Spine® training.

Biographical information from www.leebrandoninc.com

Lee Brandon has been a client and friend. I began working with Lee one year after she had won the 2001 RE/MAX Long Drive Championship and before she won the 2003 Safeway Classic. I have found her to be one of the most inspirational people I have ever met or had the pleasure to coach. Her work ethic, high moral standards, and enlightened worldview set her apart from most athletes. She is not only very bright and talented, but her heart is in the right place.

I find Lee's story particularly compelling because of the obstacles she has overcome. I believe that the heart of her story is about the process she went through to rehabilitate her arm after it had been cut off and she died on the operating table. It is always great to win, and her World Championship wins in the Long Drive are very exciting. However, the power of her story lies in how she recovered and became the Long Drive champion.

DICK FOSBURY

Richard Fosbury was born March 6, 1947, and revolutionized the high jump using a back-first technique now known as the Fosbury Flop.

Dick Fosbury first started experimenting with this new technique at age sixteen while attending high school in Medford, Oregon. He found only average success with the variety of techniques used at the time, such as the Straddle and the Scissors. The Flop tended to naturally and intuitively evolve over a few years.

As a student at Oregon State University, he won the 1968 NCAA title using his new technique, as well as the US Olympic trials. At the1968 Summer Olympics, which were held in Mexico City, he took the gold medal and set a new Olympic record (2.24 meters/7 feet 4.25 inches) in spite of the Russian and European coaches assuring him that his technique would never be successful!

Despite the initial skeptical reactions from the high jumping community, the new technique quickly gained popularity, and it is almost exclusively used by modern high jumpers. Dick is now a practicing civil engineer in Ketchum, Idaho.

My conversation with Dick covered a lot of territory—from his early high school years where he developed the Flop technique, through the 1968 summer Olympics in Mexico City where he won the gold medal with a jump of 7 feet 4.25 inches, to an interesting discussion of yoga, energy, and consciousness.

DIEGO CORRALES

I was playing golf at my home course, MountainGate Country Club, with a couple of friends. Buddy Freeman was in the foursome with his best friend, Joe Goossen. Buddy has the distinction of being the local bookie, so he knows a lot of people I would never meet. Not being much of a boxing fan at the time, I was clueless regarding Joe Goossen. Any real boxing fan knows Joe Goossen to be a great fight trainer. We all started talking about our lives, and I mentioned the book I was doing. Buddy, basically having a heart of gold, immediately said, "You should interview Diego Corrales." Again being totally clueless about the boxing world, I didn't have the slightest idea who Diego Corrales was, so I immediately said, "Great idea!" I have learned to never turn down a gift. It turned out that Joe was training Diego at his gym in the San Fernando Valley for the upcoming José Castillo fight. I went out to the gym and sat down with Diego "Chico" Corrales for about twenty minutes. Even though I felt pretty out of my element in the gym, these guys opened their hearts and homes and stopped their training to give me the opportunity to sit down and interview Diego.

Since the time of this interview, Diego tragically died in a motorcycle accident. Wikipedia.com gives the following details:

"On May 7, 2007, exactly two years to the day after his legendary fight with Castillo, Corrales was killed in a three-vehicle accident near his Las Vegas home. Corrales was riding a 2007 Suzuki GSXR 1000 motorcycle, traveling northbound on Fort Apache Road in the southwest part of the city, when he attempted to pass another vehicle at high speed. Corrales struck the back of a 1997 Honda Accord, Las Vegas police spokesman Sgt. Tracy McDonald said. 'The accident occurred at approximately 7:30 pm PDT.' McDonald said there was no outward evidence of drugs or alcohol involved. He could not say how fast the motorcycle was traveling. However, Corrales was indeed illegally drunk, with a blood alcohol level of 0.25, more than three times the legal limit of 0.08 in Nevada. Promoter Gary Shaw said, 'He's lying there as we speak with a helmet on his head under a sheet. It appears he was thrown a great distance.' Reports say that he was thrown almost the length of a football field."

It is possible that this is one of the last interviews Diego granted before his death.

Diego has a great record as a boxer. He holds multiple titles:
- International Boxing Association Super Featherweight Title
- International Boxing Association Continental Lightweight Title
- International Boxing Federation Super Featherweight Title
- World Boxing Council Lightweight Title
- World Boxing Organization Lightweight Title

He had a total of forty-four wins, thirty-three by way of knockout, and only lost four times. His fight with José Castillo was considered to be one of the greatest fights ever held. They battled ten rounds in an inside, close-up, hard-hitting bout that had Diego knocked down twice in the tenth round. After getting up after the second knockdown, he came back to deliver a technical knockout to Castillo. Just a few weeks before that fight, Diego and I were talking about one of his great moments in boxing, and he spoke about his match with Casamayor in which he was also knocked down twice in the same round and managed to get up and continue fighting. The Castillo fight was like déjà vu. I could not believe it. While I was watching this fight unfold, I kept thinking, We just talked about this; he has to remember what he said to me.

Diego was born in Sacramento, California in 1977 and was greatly influenced by his father. He died in a motorcycle accident in 2007.

Buck Rodgers

Buck Rodgers was born August 16, 1938 in Delaware, Ohio. His professional career in baseball included being a catcher, manager, and coach. As a manager, he directed three Major League teams: the Milwaukee Brewers (1980, 1980–1982), the Montreal Expos (1985–1991), and the California Angels (1991–1992, 1992–1994), compiling a career won-lost record of 784–773 (.504).

I interviewed Mr. Rodgers at his home in Orange County. We sat in his living room while his wife cooked in the kitchen. Buck was an openhearted man with warmth and sensitivity. He was generous with his time and his story.

Every individual has a unique perspective on life that appears to function as an organizing principle. This worldview serves to guide and direct their perceptions and actions. Pay attention to the theme of adjustment as it emerges from his interview. It is a very down-to-earth principle, yet it is profound in its application: the ability to adjust makes it possible to adapt to changing circumstances. It sounds rather simple, but most of us know how difficult it can be to change when we are in a familiar and comfortable pattern, even if that pattern may not be reaping the rewards we seek.

José Torres

José "Chegui" Torres, born May 3, 1936, is a Puerto Rican who is a former boxer and the first Hispanic ever to win the World Light Heavyweight Championship.

Torres was born in the Playita sector of Ponce, the same area that Sor Isolina Ferré would later call home. He joined the US Army when he was eighteen years old, where he learned to box. As Puerto Ricans have been United States citizens since 1917, he represented the country while serving in the US Army at the 1956 Olympic Games. As an Olympian, he won a silver medal as a junior middleweight.

He debuted as a professional in 1958 with a first round knockout of George Hamilton in New York. Twelve wins in a row followed, ten of them by knockout (including wins over contenders Ike Jenkins and Al Andrews), after which he was able to make his San Juan debut against Benny Paret, a World Welterweight and Middleweight Champion whose death after a fight would later go on to become one of the turning points in the history of boxing. Torres and Paret fought to a ten-round draw, and in 1960, Torres went back to campaigning in New York, where he scored three wins that year, all by decision, including two over Randy Sandy.

In 1961, Torres made his hometown debut with a four-round knockout win in a rematch with Hamilton at Ponce. He made six more fights that year, winning all of them by knockout. Throughout 1962, Torres kept his knockout streak alive with three more knockout wins, but in 1963, he suffered his first loss, being stopped in five by Cuba's Florentino Fernandez, the only boxer ever to beat Torres by a knockout as a professional. After that setback,

Torres went back to training and had one more fight that year, and that time around, he was able to beat another top contender—Don Fullmer, Gene Fullmer's brother, with a ten-round decision win in New Jersey.

In 1964, Torres beat a group of name boxers, including José Torres Gonzalez, Walker Simmons (twice), Frankie Olivera, Gomeo Brennan, and former World Middleweight Champion Carl Olson (Bobo), who he took out in one round. After this, Torres was ranked number one among light heavyweight challengers, and his title shot would arrive soon.

In 1965, it finally did. Torres fought Will Pastrano at Madison Square Garden. Pastrano was a fellow International Boxing Hall of Fame member and was the World Light Heavyweight Champion at the time. Torres became the third Puerto Rican world-boxing champion in history and first Latin American to win the Light Heavyweight title, knocking Pastrano out in round nine. He fought a non-title bout versus Tom McNeeley (father of former Mike Tyson rival Peter McNeeley) in San Juan, winning a ten-round decision.

In 1966, he successfully defended his crown three times, with fifteen round decisions over Wayne Thornton and Eddie Cotton, and a two-round knockout of Chic Calderwood. In his next defense, however, he would lose to another Hall of Fame member, Nigeria's Dick Tiger, by a decision in fifteen rounds.

In 1967, he and Tiger had a rematch, and Torres lost a fifteen-round decision again. Many fans thought he should have won it that time, and as a consequence, a large-scale riot followed the fight, with many New York City policemen called to the Madison Square Garden arena to try to calm down the fans.

After his second defeat to Tiger, Torres only fought two more times, retiring after 1969. In his years after retiring from boxing, he became a representative of the Puerto Rican community in New York, meeting political leaders, giving lectures, and becoming the New York State Athletic Commissioner from 1984 to 1988. In 1986, he was chosen to sing the United States National Anthem before the world Lightweight championship bout between Jimmy Paul and Irleis Perez in Atlantic City, New Jersey; and in 1987, he authored Fire and Fear, a book about Mike Tyson. In 1990, he became President of the World Boxing Organization, and he served as President there until 1995.

He was also a member of the International Boxing Hall of Fame, and regularly contributed a column for El Diario La Prensa, a Spanish-language newspaper in New York City. He is the author of *Sting Like a Bee*, a biography of Muhammad Ali.

Biographical Information: From Wikipedia, the free encyclopedia

I was very impressed and surprised how intelligent and articulate the boxers were. José Torres certainly exemplifies that high quality of intellect. It was my honor to have met this man and to have had the opportunity to speak with him. Once again, a boxer who made his living by fighting had the kindest, most loving disposition and was very generous with his time and life story. I never once felt an ounce of ego or personal inflation. He was humble, grateful, and sincere.

José Torres is a legend in boxing. It is a gift to get to know him. In addition to his story, he offers some astute comments on Mike Tyson and Mohammad Ali. Certainly, the central point of his interview is the importance of the intellect in boxing. He provides some valuable insight as to why it is important to box intelligently and not just be a strong bull.

On January 19, 2009, Mr. Torres died of a heart attack in his home at Ponce, Puerto Rico.

Trey Waltke

Trey Waltke (born March 16, 1955) is an American former professional tennis player whose career spanned more than a decade during the 1970s and 1980s.

Waltke came from Los Angeles, California, and although often going up against players as an underdog, he was one of the few players to beat John McEnroe and Jimmy Connors in the same year. During a first-round match at Wimbledon in 1983 against Stan Smith, Waltke caused a stir when he donned 1920s era long flannel pants, a white buttoned-down long-sleeved shirt, and a necktie for a belt. He beat Smith in five sets but lost to Ivan Lendl in the second round.

From Wikipedia, the free encyclopedia

Index

E

F

T

www.ingramcontent.com/pod-product-compliance
Lightning Source LLC
Chambersburg PA
CBHW021220090426
42740CB00006B/304